A PRIMER OF COOKING

AND HOUSEKEEPING

BY ELIZABETH COOPER

Cover Art: "Lady Violetta and the Knave Observe the Tarts" by Maxfield Parrish (ills. from "The Knave of Hearts.")

Copyright © 1979 Ross Books

Library of Congress Cataloging in Publication Data

Cooper, Elizabeth, 1940-
   A primer of cooking and housekeeping.

   Includes index.
   1. Cookery. 2. Home economics. I. Title.
TX715.C7863   641.5   78-25791
ISBN 0-89496-015-6

ROSS BOOKS

P.O.BOX 4340
BERKELEY, CALIF.
94704

FOREWORD

This book is intended to fill a gap that most people find when they look through today's cook books. Most of the cook books you find on the market are aimed at specialized dishes and almost all cook books assume you have a fundamental knowledge of cooking. This fundamental knowledge, which is so easily overlooked, can go a long way in helping you create your own recipes. For example, you may find books on how to cook fancy cakes, but what is the *basic* recipe for making cakes? With this understanding, you can improvise and create your own cakes. The same is true with cooking every daily meal you have. It is the purpose of this book to provide you with just that information and we start by assuming you know nothing. We assume someone has been feeding you all your life and now you find yourself on your own (you poor dear).

First, we will have a short basic discussion on the philosophy of why you have been fed the way you have. This will give you an idea of the scheme of things. We will then go through the kitchen and make sure you are set up properly (and not collecting junk). Then we will go through the three main meals of the day showing you how to cook the most common meals you daily encounter in a way that will leave you not only able to make all your common recipes, but able to change the recipes so you can create your own dishes. Plenty of basic recipes for each meal will be given. Hints will be given at the end of some sections on how to make things a little easier, quicker, etc. When you finish this book, you will have everything you need to create normal and even fancy daily meals for yourself and your family.

The last section is on housekeeping. I know nobody can tell you how to keep your house (and no one should), but there are many hints that will make cleaning, mending, etc. much easier as well as save you money. So the housekeeping section (as well as the whole book) will serve as a handbook, of a sort, to help make your daily household living a little more pleasant.

TABLE OF CONTENTS

IN AND OUT

OF

THE KITCHEN

THE MEAL SCHEME

You will find it hard to improve upon the French theory of meals which recognizes as a serious consideration only one meal of the three. The French have coffee or chocolate and rolls for breakfast, combinations of appetizing trifles for lunch, and at night, when they are hungry and unhurried, they have a very substantial dinner.

This plan is good for the digestion because it gives the body rest before each big meal. It is economical, because it concentrates expense upon dinner alone (presupposing that lunch may be built on dinner leftovers). If thoughtfully worked out, it is also the most time saving plan possible for the housekeeper. Planning your meal is very important and a few moments' thought can save hours of cooking. After you have read this book and are ready to make some meals, sit down *the night before* and think out your next day's meals carefully. Make sure you are making best use of your time and cooking space. Make sure you are arranging your cooking around the time you have available. For example, if you are going to be busy in the afternoon, the meat for dinner, and the potatoes with it, may be cooked in the morning. Save oven space and time: if the meat is to be baked, a baked dessert may be mixed up and put in the oven at the same time. Write down your schedule if you are going to be very busy the next day. A few minutes thought the night before makes a world of difference the next day.

11.

EASY WAYS AROUND THE KITCHEN

You will find out through experience that the only way to hurry in the kitchen is to be neat. Not excessively neat. Just neat enough to pick up after yourself. For instance, after beating an egg, hold the egg beater under cold water immediately and then under hot water (it only takes a minute). Dry it. Put it in it's drawer. When you take a little corn starch or spice from a box, put the box back in it's place automatically. Set the butter back in the icebox after you have taken out what you need. When you have finished mixing up a cake, put the mixing bowl and spoons under cold and then hot water. Wash them and put them away. When you empty a saucepan or a frying pan, put it in the sink and fill it with cold water. You will find it much easier to wash later on than if you had left it to dry.

It is important to wash your pots and pans thoroughly. If you put them away sloppily washed, you will have to rinse them out before you can use them again. A bread board put away with flour sticking to it will be too uneven to roll pie dough on the next time you need it.

If you look ahead, in managing kitchen affairs, you will find yourself inventing all sorts of schemes to save time without sacrificing neatness. You will spread towels or newspapers on your kitchen table when you cut cabbage or pare potatoes. Then this paper may be gathered up with the scraps in a heap and thrown in the garbage can. This is a much shorter operation than clearing off the table and wiping it with a cloth. You will put food away, as often as possible, in a

12.

receptacle that can go either on top of the stove or in the oven so that you will not have to soil another dish to reheat it. You will have a place for every cooking utensil. Putting an article in it's place doesn't even take a minute. Finding it there when you need it in a hurry is a great satisfaction as well as time saved.

There is a difference between laziness and good planning. It is not laziness, for example, to drain your dishes instead of drying them. If each dish is washed with soapy water, rinsed, then set in a draining rack with boiling water finally poured over the whole rack, the moisture will dry by evaporation in a few minutes leaving the dish really cleaner and shinier than if it had been mopped over with a half-damp cloth. Glassware and silverware, however, must be dried or glassware will look cloudy and silverware will tarnish.

I am sure the idea is clear by now. Every kitchen is different. You will have to find what works best around your kitchen but the basic principle is as old as the hills and known the world over. Before you start any meal or work in the kitchen, think it through. Then you will be able to work much more quickly (because you know what you are doing) and you will be more economical in your work for the same reason.

It's your kitchen

Experiment

SETTING UP: KITCHEN UTENSILS

Exactly what utensils do you need for *your* kitchen? Do you really know? Well, neither does anybody else. Everybody's style is different. Let's start with just what's necessary. A few basics are all you need to get started. This list should do it:

Large frying pan with lid.   *Cooking utensil set (to hang on wall):*
Small frying pan   *Fork*
Double boiler   *Ladle*
Large pot   *Slotted spoon*
Small pot (3–4 cup size)   *Pancake turner*
                              Spatula

Egg beater
Measuring spoons
Measuring cup   *Roasting pan*
Rubber spatula   *Covered casserole dish*
Can opener   *Square baking pan*
Flour sifter   *Set of three mixing bowls*
Grater
Strainer   *Foil wrap*
Thick pot holders   *Plastic wrap*

As your cooking style develops and your skills grow, you'll have a better idea of what to look for in more specialized tools. Meanwhile, if you don't have an item called for in a recipe, don't panic.

Improvise.

14.

For instance, a roasting pan turned upside down makes a good cookie tray. A cast iron skillet can double as a roasting pan for chickens, hams and roasts. Add a piece of foil for a lid and it becomes a covered casserole. A tall jar or bottle can roll out dough as well as any rolling pin and a glass becomes a cookie cutter. A strainer can sift flour or serve as a collander to drain noodles, lettuce, whatever, and a fork can mash potatoes.

Take a hard look at appliances before you buy. Most of them are designed to save labor but that doesn't mean they will save *you* labor. An electric can opener is only great if you have a whole lot of cans to open. Blenders can do fantastic tricks but you have to take the trouble to learn the tricks. A toaster oven is fun but if everybody in the house starts using it for every little snack, your electricity bill can go up and you might be eating too much between meals. Electric frying pans, slow cooking pots, juicers, yogurt makers, coffee grinders, food processors, etc., are invaluable aids if they are *actually* part of your cooking style. If they aren't, they become expensive dust catchers and just one more thing that takes up counter space.

Once you decide you want a certain appliance, check out the different brands. Talk to people who have one. Find out how the consumer magazines rate the item and the different brands. A little homework before you buy can keep you from getting stuck with something you really don't need.

One more point. A kitchen that's disorganized causes more frustration than a recipe that's hard to follow. Keeping utensils next to your work area saves steps. Hanging pots and utensils on hooks or peg board makes them easier to use and saves fatigue. An icebox that's too far from either sink or stove can double the time you have to spend in the kitchen.

It's not necessary to do all your organizing at once. In fact, it may take time to discover what kind of organization works best for you but try to do as much as you can as soon as you can. It's up to you to make your kitchen work.

KITCHEN CLEANING HINTS

In the housekeeping section are hints on general house-keeping but here are a few hints for just the kitchen.

THE REFRIGERATOR: Open refrigerator doors seldom and keep them open as short a time as possible. Cover everything placed in the refrigerator with the exception of eggs. Do not pack the shelves too closely. Allow the air to circulate. Never permit open bottles or cans of liquids or moist materials to stand uncovered in the refrigerator. Clean the refrigerator once a month. Wash it out quickly with a lukewarm solution of bicarbonate of soda. Wash the ice trays occasionally with boiling water to which a little bicarbonate of soda has been added. Also, if you wish, a box of bicarbonate of soda, left open, may be placed in the refrigerator to help eliminate odors. This should be changed every month at cleaning time.

THE STOVE: It's amazing how much you can learn from the manufacturer's manual and they cost very little. If you don't have one, call your local store and order one. It takes only a minute and is well worth the trouble. If you have a gas stove, always remember in lighting it to hold the match over the gas burner and then slowly turn on the gas. If you turn the gas on too quickly, the explosion causes the gas meter to jump and thus your gas bill is increased. It is also surprising how much you can reduce your gas consumption in one year by turning off the gas before, instead of after, removing utensils. Just be

16.

conscious of when the gas is on (ie, do not leave a burner lit because you expect to use it in the future). A cone-shaped culinary bottle brush is handy to have for cleaning the stove since there are a lot of hard to get at places. They not only take off all the grease but they keep your hands from getting grimy too.

If your kitchen stove is rusted, go over the surface with a soft cloth dipped in vinegar. If necessary, repeat the process and the spots will go away.

Should your stove catch fire, throw salt or soda on the flames. Do not attempt to throw water if grease is burning as the fire can easily spread.

SLATE: Frequently you will find simple cleaning helpers that you wish you had on hand not available. Somewhere in your kitchen, you should have a pad of paper and a pencil or a child's blackboard and chalk hung on the wall (*Not* in a drawer. Stick it in a drawer and you'll forget it). If you can jot down food and kitchen supplies you need as you think of them, you will save a great deal of time and effort later. You never remember everything you need if you wait until the last minute.

CLEANLINESS IN WASHING: The best way to assure sanitation in washing is by the use of plenty of soap and hot water and by starting each washing operation with clean wash cloths and towels. Have a few dishcloths which are to be used for no other purpose than washing dishes. Have others for wiping up spilled foods, etc. This will minimize the possibility of contamination.

17.

Dish cloths should be regularly washed in hot suds, scalded, and hung up to dry. They should always be sweet and clean.When washing greasy dishes or utensils, add a few drops of liquid ammonia to the water. Lemon juice can also be used to cut grease in dishwater. Lemon juice may also be applied to the hands after washing and will keep them soft and clean.

Remember to keep the sink and drain cleaned. Pouring hot salt water into the sink after washing will keep the grease from any build up it may be starting to do.

GLASSWARE: When washing glassware, dip the pieces in warm water so they will be wet on the inside and outside at the same time. Unequal expansion of the glass caused by one part being suddenly overheated can cause breaks. When washing, glassware should be done first, as the dishwater is cleanest then and transparent glass will show spots more easily than other materials. Glassware can be made to sparkle if washed in warm, soapy water and a brush used for cut and ornamental parts. A few drops of vinegar can be added to the rinsing water to prevent spotting. Baking soda is also excellent for cleaning glassware. You can simply pour a bit into each glass and rub with a little water and rinse. The glasses will sparkle and be free of spots frequently left by soap.

When glass bottles, jars or even earthen vessels have a musty and disagreeable odor, fill them with cold water in which soda has been dissolved. Let them sit for an hour or overnight and rinse with warm water.

An old method to successfully mend glass (if you don't have special glue around) is to melt a small quantity of pulverized alum in an old spoon. Before it hardens, rub the alum over the pieces to be united, press them together and set aside

18.

to dry. If it is difficult to keep the pieces in position, try holding them together with adhesive tape. When the article is thoroughly dry and secure, carefully pull off the tape. They will not come apart even when washed in hot water.

CLEANING GREASY PANS: When you wash the pots and pans, place the greasy skillet or roaster on the stove. Pour into it a cup or so of soapy dishwater. Let it come to a boil, simmer a few minutes, and the washing can now be easily completed in the dish pan.

Another method is to pour a few drops of ammonia into every greasy roasting pan immediately after cooking in it. Then fill it with hot water. If left to stand like this until time to wash, the work of cleaning will be half done.

When pouring out the grease from pans, you cannot pour into the kitchen sink without fear of clogging the pipes. Either pour the grease in an old can to be thrown out with the trash or place a piece of newspaper in the sink strainer before pouring greasy water into the sink. The newspaper will hold the grease and keep the pipes from clogging.

COFFEE POTS: To clean out a coffee pot, place a tablespoon of soda into it and fill with water. Boil for twenty minutes. Then pour out soda and water and boil with fresh water.

When storing metal coffee pots or tea kettles for a while, they are likely to become musty. This is prevented by dropping a lump of sugar into the pot before putting away. The sugar will absorb the moisture and keep it off the metal.

ALUMINUM: To clean aluminum when you have no special cleanser at hand, dip a cut lemon in salt and clean vigorously. Rinse at once. Do not use salt alone, as plain alkali is not good

19.

for this metal. Of course, wire or plastic wool will remove all rough places and discolorations due to burned food.

WAFFLE IRONS: An electric waffle iron may be kept bright and shining, inside and out, with ordinary baking soda. Of course, water must not be used for fear of injuring the heating elements. Simply apply the soda dry with a dry brush and scrub. The discoloration will quickly disappear.

BRASS AND COPPER: For cleaning brass and copper if you do not have a special paste on hand, use salt mixed with an equal part of flour and vinegar (enough to make a paste). Let this stand for an hour or so, then rub off with a soft cloth. Afterwards, wash and use a soft brush for places that cannot be reached with a cloth. Then polish to a shine.

ENAMELWARE: Enamelware may be cleaned by dipping a wet cloth into baking soda and rubbing it on the utensil. Do not spare the soda. Never put soda and water into an enameled saucepan that has been burned. This will remove the burned particles of food, but it will also make the saucepan likely to burn again the next time time you use it. Use salt instead of soda. Fill the pan with cold water, leave until the next day, then slowly bring the water to a boil. The pan will be quite clean and there will be no bad effect.

IVORY: When ivory ornaments become yellow, wash them well in soap and water. Then place them while still wet in the sunshine. Wet them with soapy water for two or three days, several times a day, still keeping them in the sunshine. Wash again and they will be perfectly white.

SILVER: Silver may be cleaned by soaking for several hours or overnight in thick sour milk if you don't have any silver polish handy. Be sure the milk covers it. When clean and bright, take out and wash in soapy hot water. Then scald with hot water and wipe with soft towel. The results are pleasantly surprising. Silver is brighter if it is wiped directly from clean, hot, slightly soapy water.

Here is a way to remove scratches from silver. Mix enough putty powder with a little olive oil to make a paste. Rub this paste on the silver with a soft cloth. Polish with chamois. The scratches will disappear.

Never wrap silver in bleached flannel. Wrap it in unbleached flannel. The sulphur used in bleaching flannel will tarnish silver. Also, a few pieces of camphor placed in the drawer where silver is kept will keep it from tarnishing by absorbing the moisture.

STEEL: When steel becomes rusty, rub it with a piece of emery paper that has been dipped in turpentine. Polish with a fresh piece of emery paper and you will be delighted with the result.

CLEANING KITCHEN TABLE: To bleach a discolored wooden kitchen table, cutting block, etc., scrub it with a solution made of one teaspoon of household bleach to one cup of hot water applied with a cloth. The kitchen breadboard or anything wooden should also regularly be cleaned in this manner.

PRESERVING KNIVES: Each time after using a knife for any purpose, it should be rinsed, cleaned, run through a sharpener, dried and put away. Acids from meats as well as citrus fruits are extremely corrosive (even to stainless steel) and will pit the

21.

metal. The life of your knives will be greatly increased with a small amount of care.

NEWSPAPER IN KITCHEN: Keep a pile of newspapers in the kitchen cut in half. Sheets will save much work in cleaning the stove, catching peelings, wiping burns from kettles, spilled food from the stove and cleaning the sink.

AID ON GARBAGE CAN: Put a clothespin through the handle of the garbage can so that you can open it in cold, frosty weather without having your hands stick.

22.

BREAKFAST

BREAKFAST

It has to be cooked fast, in most homes, and eaten fast too. Breakfast is not a lukewarm meal. Its function is to stir the appetite and satisfy the hunger that perhaps does not consciously exist.

There are two types of dishes at breakfast: hot and cold. Try to have the hot dish (cooked cereal, bacon & eggs, etc.) very hot. Have the fruit and cream, etc., very cold. If you are serving someone, keep the hot things hot with dishcovers and the cold things cold by leaving them in the icebox until needed.

Although coffee (or chocolate) and rolls for breakfast is an ideal working basis (complying with the French theory that breakfast should be as light as possible), it will not do for the person who goes out for a hard day's manual work. In contrast to it, however, is the heavy breakfast of oatmeal, chops, fried potatoes, hot bread and coffee. This sort of heavy breakfast is not only an unfair burden on the housekeeping end of things but it is too much for the digestion. It can make a person sluggish for part of the day, among other things.

As a compromise, breakfast might include a fruit course and then either a substantial cereal course or a light hot course of eggs ham, wheat cakes, fish or bacon and then coffee with rolls or toast.

Now we will go through how to make some of the standard breakfast dishes.

27.

BASIC HOT BEVERAGES

Here is how to make some of your typical breakfast beverages if they are not the instant kind.

COFFEE

Have the coffee ground of medium fineness and, as soon as you get home from the store with it, empty it from the paper or cardboard container into an airtight container.

To make coffee (other than instant), put in the pot a heaping tablespoon for each person to be served. Follow this with as many cups of cold water. Use a standard half–pint measuring cup or glass. You can add an egg shell crushed up for the purpose of clearing the liquid if you want. Put this over a brisk fire. When it has come to a boil, turn the flame down low and simmer the coffee for at least five minutes. The whole operation for five or six portions of coffee will take about twenty minutes at most.

TEA

Tea ball tea is simple. Heat the water to the boiling point and pour it over a tea ball half filled with tea in each cup separately. To steep tea, put in a tea pot which has been rinsed out with boiling water half a teaspoon of tea for each person. Pour about a cupful of boiling water over this, cover, and let stand for two minutes. Then add as many more cups of boiling water as are needed.

COCOA

For each person to be served, measure into a saucepan a level teaspoon each of cocoa and sugar. Blend these with a little milk. Then add a cup of milk for each portion. Bring to a boil over a low fire and serve immediately.

EGGS

Ideally, eggs should be cooked delicate (never leathery). They should also be cooked with seasoning and, whenever possible, garnished with toast or bacon, tomato, lettuce or whatever to increase their appeal.

When deciding how many eggs to use for an omelet or for scrambled eggs, add one egg for each person plus two for the pot. The number of poached or fried eggs to be cooked depends upon the appetite of the people being served.

FRIED EGGS

Fried eggs, cooked soft, are the most universally popular. Have butter, bacon, or other meat drippings slowly melting in a frying pan while you break the eggs into a wide shallow bowl (taking care not to break the yolks). Then gently slide all the eggs into the pan and turn the fire up under it. Salt and pepper each egg. With a spatula, begin separating the eggs. As soon as the whites are fairly set, turn each egg and cook it for a half minute on the other side. Then put it on a hot plate to serve.

OMELET

There is nothing to be afraid of in omelet making except having too hot a fire under the skillet. Put a tablespoon of cooking fat into the pan and let it melt. Meanwhile, beat the yolks and the whites of the eggs in separate bowls. Add to the

30.

yolks a tablespoon of water for each yolk (milk tends to make the eggs heavier). Season yolks and whites. Lastly, add the whites to the yolks stirring gently until they are blended. Pour the mixture into the frying pan. Let it cook for a few minutes, occasionally testing it by lifting up an edge with a spatula to see if the under side is beginning to brown. When it is light brown, add to the omelet any extra feature you may like. Lima beans, grated cheese, rice, or a few tablespoons of tomato sauce are often used. Take the frying pan off the fire and set it in the oven (under the broiler if you have one) until the top is set. Then take the pan out of the oven, turn one half of the omelet over the other half and serve. Always make sure that an omelet is loosened from the sides of the pan before turning out. Hold the omelet pan firmly while slipping the omelet onto the platter.

SCRAMBLED EGGS

Scrambled eggs are not be literally scrambled. Scrambling makes them dry and rubbery.

Break into a bowl the eggs to be cooked and beat them. Add salt and pepper and one tablespoon of water or milk for each egg. Melt half a tablespoon of butter or bacon fat in a frying pan. With a slow fire under the pan, pour the eggs into it and let them alone for the first minute of cooking. Then, with a spoon, gently work at them from time to time. Lift them from the bottom of the pan to the top while keeping them in one mass. When there is no liquid part left at the edge of the pan, the eggs are done. They will be soft, well moistened, and delicate.

POACHED EGGS

The advantage of poaching eggs rather than frying them lies in the fact that fats and calories are reduced. Poaching also offers the possibility of enhancing the flavor of the eggs (by simmering in a savory liquid, the eggs will absorb part of that liquid). Eggs may be given a meat flavor by poaching them in gravy or bouillon. They may be made rich by poaching them in a little tomato sauce with spice in it or in a cheese cream sauce.

To poach eggs, heat the liquid to be used to the boiling point and gently submerge the eggs into the liquid (using a poaching ring if possible). Turn off the fire and leave it covered. In four or five minutes the eggs will be done with a white film over each one. Do not try to poach eggs by putting them in lukewarm or slightly boiling water. The water must be rapidly boiling so that the white is cooked at once (otherwise the egg spreads in the water).

STEAMED EGGS

A quick way to cook eggs for individual servings (as for a tray breakfast), is in small casseroles. Drop one or two eggs into each casserole, which has been buttered. Season with salt and pepper. Put a little butter on top of each egg. Set the casseroles in a shallow tin baking dish half full of hot water. Put a lid over the casseroles. Cook over a brisk fire until the whites are set.

32.

BREAKFAST MEATS

Pork is most frequently prepared as a breakfast meat and the most important consideration to remember in its preparation is to be certain it is thoroughly cooked. Pork can contain disease and therefore must be completely cooked to eliminate any potential hazard.

BACON

To prepare crisp bacon, it is necessary to have the frying pan hot when you lay the strips of bacon in it. With a fork, turn each slice as soon as the under side is seared. Then lower the flame under the pan and keep turning the bacon until each piece is a light brown. Drain off the grease from the pan into a container (ready to be used as cooking fat). Let the bacon lie for a minute in the dry pan or drain on paper. Then serve it. Cook two or three slices for each person.

HAM

Before cooking a slice of ham, cut off the brown rind along the side opposite the fatty side. Leave all the fat on. Then, with a sharp knife, make short incisions along the lean side. This will keep the ham from curling while it cooks.

Have a hot frying pan ready. Put the ham in, leave it until one side is white, then turn it. Turn two or three times, with the fire high, until both sides are beginning to brown. Then turn down the fire, cover the frying pan and let the ham cook

33.

slowly for at least fifteen minutes. At the end of this time, turn the fire up long enough to complete the browning. A small slice of ham will be about the right quantity for two people.

SAUSAGE

Fresh country sausage is to be made into small flat cakes about an inch and a half in diameter, pressed into compactness, and fried in a hot frying pan without any other grease than its own. Turn the cakes often and let them cook not more than fifteen minutes in all. Squeeze a few drops of lemon juice over each cake before serving.

Smoked sausage or frankfurters should be slit down one side and fried over a slow fire until the skin is crisp and brown.

HOT CAKES

There are several points to be remembered about making hot cakes:

Have a steady heat under the griddle. Get the griddle to the point where grease dropped on it will sizzle. Then turn the fire down low enough simply to keep it at this temperature.

Put the cake batter, when mixed, into a pitcher and pour it on the griddle from this. This will make the cakes uniform in size and shape. It will also do away with the messiness dropping batter from a spoon.

If the cake batter does not sizzle when dropped on the griddle, the griddle is not hot enough.

Turn the cakes when two or more bubbles show on the upper side.

Any cake batter may be mixed up the night before and refrigerated overnight.

FLANNEL CAKES

Beat up one egg, well salted, in a mixing bowl. In a half pint measuring cup, put half a teaspoon of soda. Fill up the cup with sour milk and stir until the milk is smooth. Add to this the egg and stir into the mixture a half pint of sifted flour in which half a teaspoon of baking powder has been mixed. Stir until smooth.

This quantity will serve two people.

BUCKWHEAT CAKES

These must be made the night before. Put three cups of buckwheat in a mixing bowl. Add one tablespoon of wheat flour, a pinch of salt, a tablespoon of molasses (to make the cakes brown), half a yeast cake crumbled up, and enough warm water to make the whole thing into a rather thin batter. Beat the mixture thoroughly until all the ingredients are blended. Cover it with a piece of cloth and leave it in a cool place overnight. If it is too thick in the morning to pour easily from the pitcher, thin it with milk.

There will be enough batter to serve two people for several successive mornings. Refrigerate between meals in a covered container.

Some sort of honey or syrup should be served with hot cakes. Maple syrup is delicious, but quite expensive. There are a number of good brands of manufactured syrups on the market (which are combinations of maple syrup and granulated sugars), and are less costly than pure maple syrup.

Lacking any of these, one can make a good syrup by boiling half a cupful of brown sugar with half a cup of cold water for a few minutes (until thickened slightly). Add a drop each of vanilla and maple extracts. If the syrup remaining after the meal is to be stored, the addition of two tablespoons of corn syrup will prevent it from crystalizing.

36.

HOT BREADS

The types of hot breads you can make are endless. They are usually present at most breakfast meals. They are something that is easy to hold in the hand, never a meal in themselves, and always substantial enough to round off a meal. We will go through some of the most common kinds of hot breads assuming you are not buying one of the instant mixes.

MUFFINS

Before starting to mix them, heat the oven to 200 degrees.

Put two tablespoons of butter in one of the compartments of a muffin pan and set this over a low flame to melt. While it is melting, break an egg into a bowl, add a tablespoon of sugar, stir together, add a cup of milk (or half milk and half water) and add two cups of sifted flour. The sifted flour should have three teaspoons of baking powder and a teaspoon of salt in it. Last, add the melted butter. Beat for a minute or two and pour out by spoonfuls into the muffin pan. Have each compartment not more than two thirds full. Bake in the slow oven which has been heating until the muffins rise. This will take about ten minutes. Then turn the fire up and let the muffins cook to a delicate brown. Twenty minutes in all should be long enough to cook them. Makes eight muffins.

BISCUITS

Preheat oven to 450 degrees. Into a mixing bowl, sift three cups of flour, four teaspoons of baking powder and one teaspoon of salt. In the center of this, put three teaspoons of butter, lard, or any good vegetable fat. Work the flour and fat with your fingers until the fat is distributed through the flour. Make a hole in the center of the flour and pour three forths of a cup of cold water into it. Work this with the flour until you have the whole thing into a soft ball. Remember, biscuits too wet to roll on the board will be very light. They may be dropped from the spoon or molded by the hand if flour is dropped on them and on the hands.

Now, on a thickly floured board, roll the dough into a sheet about an inch thick. Cut the sheet with a biscuit cutter or the top of a small glass into circles. As a variation, you can roll the dough thinner than usual and use two cuts for one biscuit (having one on top of the other). Made this way, the biscuits will break open more evenly and readily. They will also be daintier.

Place biscuits on a greased cookie tray and bake in a 400 degree oven until brown. This makes eight biscuits.

POPOVERS

Heat oven to 450 degrees. Grease six compartments of the muffin pan. In each compartment put a dab of butter. In a mixing bowl, beat one egg and add, while continuing to beat, one cupful of milk and one cup of sifted flour plus a pinch of salt. Pour the batter into the pan and place on top of each dab of butter. Cook 15 minutes. Then turn the fire down to 350 degrees and let them get cooked through. The whole baking will take from twenty to thirty five minutes.

CORNBREAD

In a mixing bowl, stir together a cup of corn meal, half a cup of flour, one third of a cup of sugar, a half teaspoon of salt and two teaspoons of baking powder. Beat up one egg, in a separate bowl, and add to it a cup of milk. Add the eggs and milk to the dry ingredients, beat for a few minutes and then pour into a loaf cake pan. Bake in a slow oven until they are brown and firm. This quantity will make enough for four people.

TOAST

Use your older bread first in making toast. It is more economical and sometimes even better eating.

People always make more toast than they need. Save those extra pieces. Bread crusts or crumbs can be browned in a very slow oven and be put away to be used in Au Gratin dishes (if they are treated in this way they will not mildew). Another use for leftover toast is french toast. Dip the toast in a better of egg and milk (try ¼ cup milk to two eggs). Add a pinch of spice (nutmeg or cinnamon) to the egg mix. Brown in a pan with margarine or butter. Serve with syrup.

MARMALADE

There are many kinds of jams you can make and we are going to do marmalade. It's good to make your own marmalade not just for the satisfaction of having your own home made jam, but it is also economical (it gives you a way to use up extra fruit you have lying around).

CANNED FRUIT MARMALADE

Peaches, pineapple, pears, berries, or cherries may be used for this. If cherries are used, first stone them.

Drain a cupful of fruit and cut it into small pieces. Add to it the juice of one lemon and a cup of sugar. Cook over a medium fire for about twenty minutes. Let it cool before serving at breakfast.

ORANGE MARMALADE

Wash one orange and one lemon. With a sharp knife, cut each piece of fruit (rind, white skin and all) into shreds. Measure the result and put it into a saucepan with three full measures of water to each one of shredded fruit. Set this away to soak until the same hour the next day. Then measure the mixture and to every cupful allow the same amount of sugar (adding one extra cup of sugar at the last). Put the saucepan over a moderate fire and cook until the mixture seems thick. A good test of this is that it will drop from the spoon in two places at the same time. Then pour it into hot jelly glasses that are standing in a pan of hot water. This quantity of marmalade should fill seven glasses.

CEREALS

There are a large number of hot cereals on the market today and almost all can be prepared quickly from directions on the package.

People always make too much hot cereal. Here is a way you can save that cereal. Put it in the refrigerator and the next morning it should be cold and firm enough to handle as one mass. Flatten it and put it carefully in a frying pan with several tablespoons of butter. Sift brown sugar over the top and turn the cereal with a spatula. Sugar the other side. Make the mass of cereal sort of flat like a pancake. Brown with a hot fire. Serve with syrup. You can save your extra cereal this way and not have to serve the same cereal over again to people at breakfast.

LUNCH

LUNCH

Lunch may be the one unplanned meal. Its elements are simple because lunch is the meal of tidbits and leftovers. Leftovers, no matter what you do with them, are leftovers. So don't feel bad when the people you are feeding recognize what it is that they are eating. Instead, concentrate on simply fixing leftovers in a way that makes people look forward to eating them. You do this by taking them apart and putting them together in an interesting way.

Taking them apart means chopping, shredding, grinding, mincing and/or separating the meat from the bone and gristle.

Putting them together means combining them with other ingredients to make an interesting dish. Eggs, gravy and cream sauce are the ingredients most often used to combine leftovers. With eggs you can turn them into souffles, timbales and fritters.

EGG COMBINATIONS

Eggs, gravy and cream sauce are the ingredients most often used to combine leftovers. The variety is endless and we will do some of the most common ones. With eggs you can turn them into souffles, timbales and fritters in the following manner:

SOUFFLE

The idea of souffle making is to swell the amount of your food material by combining it with beaten egg, then baking it in a moderate oven (like a cake) until it rises and browns on top. It will bake in about twenty minutes. A souffle is usually made in a straight sided clay pot but an enameled baking pan or even a tin one will do. Grease the pan first.

As many eggs as you like may be used to increase the bulk of the dish. For a rule of thumb, to one cup of chopped meat, or cooked vegetables, or flaked salmon, two eggs will be about the suitable proportion.

To make the souffle, beat the yolks of the eggs until they are stiff (drop a pinch of salt in before starting to beat). Add the leftover material. Beat the egg whites until they are foamy and gently fold them into the egg yolk mixture. Half a cup of milk should be added if a dry absorbent material such as rice or potatoes is used. Bake as described above. The souffle will serve three.

48.

TIMBALES

A timbale is an elaboration of a souffle and an adaptation of it to individual serving. It combines left over food materials of all kinds with egg not to increase the bulk, but simply to hold it together. It is usually very highly seasoned and made of two or more different base ingredients which are mashed before being combined. Each timbale is baked in a separate greased baking dish and when done is emptied out upside down on the serving plate. It may be served hot or cold and with or without sauce.

Baked beans and ground cooked ham make a very appetizing timbale combination. Mash the beans into a paste, add the ham, a few drops of lemon juice and a quarter of a teaspoon of prepared mustard. Add to this one beaten egg for each cupful of beans, as much ham as you like, and stir the mixture. Divide it among the desired number of baking dishes. Tin gelatine molds will do very well instead of china or earthenware dishes. Set the dishes in a shallow baking dish containing hot water. Put this in a moderately hot oven and bake until the timbales are solid with a little brown on top. By running a blunt bladed knife around the edges and underneath, you can easily remove the timbales.

Salmon or other fish timbales are perhaps improved by being served cold with a slice of lemon on top of each or with one of the fish sauces. If it is to be served cold, let the timbale stand in its baking dish until it is ready to be served. It will then come out of the mold more easily.

49.

FRITTERS

In fritters, which are really a form of batter cake, the eggs are used for the purpose of holding the ingredients together. Fritters are the simplest egg combination of the three but the most limited (for only certain base ingredients are suitable for fritters). Canned corn, chopped ham (or other cooked meat), rice, mashed potatoes, shredded cooked green peppers, bananas, apples, pineapple and peaches virtually complete the list. The last four are recommended for desserts and should be sprinkled with powdered sugar.

To make fritters, beat one egg for every cup of base ingredients. Season the egg with salt and pepper and add the left over food to it. Stir in two tablespoons of flour mixed with two teaspoons of baking powder and two tablespoons of milk. If canned corn is used, no milk need be added. Beat the mixture until it bubbles and then drop it, a tablespoon at a time, into a frying pan in which some cooking fat has been melted. Have the fire under the pan low until the fritters have begun to cook through, then increase to moderate heat. Turn each fritter when the under side is brown. Pile, at one side of the pan, those that are done, while the rest are being fried. One cup of material will make enough fritters for three.

There is an Italian dish of fried vegetables that belongs in the list of fritters. Its name is *fritto misto* and it is an attractive form in which to serve assorted left over vegetables. Suppose in the refrigerator there are the following: a dab of spaghetti cooked with tomato sauce, a few slices of beets, a quarter of a cup of mashed potato and some peas. This is a good foundation for fritto misto.

Put all these things into separate heaps on a big platter or bread board. Chop the spaghetti and the beets fine. Mash the peas and keep each vegetable separate. Then beat up an egg in a bowl and pour in some bread crumbs into a shallow dish. Make each vegetable into two or three small compact rolls or cakes. Dip each roll, first into the egg, then into the bread crumbs, using a sieve spoon. Fry the rolls in hot melted butter or other cooking fat until they are brown all over. Serve them with hot tomato soup poured over them for sauce.

51.

HASH AND STEWS

When there is left over gravy and cooked meat with potatoes available, you can make a main dish which may be put together with gravy instead of with eggs. This will be a stew or hash which can be baked or browned on top of the stove. The secret of good hashes and stews lies in the preparation of the meat. There must be no gristle or fat on it. It must be cut or chopped into small uniformly shaped pieces. Mix it thoroughly with the gravy before cooking. Season it with something tangible (minced raw onion, a teaspoon of worcestershire sauce or a pinch of powdered sage).

To make a stew, put the meat, mixed with gravy and seasoned, in a frying pan. Add half a cup of potatoes and any other vegetable which you may have on hand. If there is no cooked potato and you want the stew to be bulkier, add one raw potato cut into very small pieces. Season, add enough cold water to come half way up the material, and cover the pan with a tight fitting lid. Cook over a medium fire for fifteen minutes.

Hash may be baked or fried. Prepare the meat as for a stew (chopping it a little finer, however) and add cooked potatoes or any other vegetables desired. Raw potatoes must not be used. Melt a tablespoon of cooking fat in the frying pan and lay the hash in it while flattening it down into a solid mass. If you are going to do the cooking on top of the stove, turn the flame down low, cover the pan and let the bottom side of the hash get brown. Then, with a broad spatula, turn it while keeping it in one mass if possible. When both sides are brown it is done.

If you prefer to bake the hash, add half a cupful of hot water to the pan, leave it uncovered, and put it in a 350 degree oven. After about ten minutes, take the pan out, turn the hash, add another half cup of water and return to the oven. Bake until the other side is brown. It is obvious that baking is a little more trouble and its advantage is that it gets the hash drier than frying.

CREAMED DISHES

Cream sauce is the third combining agency to be used in putting leftovers together. It is particularly good for potatoes, salted meats and fish.

It is very easy to make a good cream sauce. Remember to use approximately as much flour as butter and for the ordinary sauce take a cup of milk (or half milk and half water if necessary) to one tablespoon each of butter and flour. Melt the butter over a slow fire, add the flour and stir until it and the butter are smooth. Slowly begin adding the milk, stirring constantly until thoroughly blended. Continue stirring after all of the milk is in. When the sauce begins to thicken, add the left over materials to be used. Season with salt and pepper and serve when just at the boiling point.

Creamed potatoes by themselves are obviously not a very good thing to have for the main lunch dish. So put something in with them, to give them tang. Some chopped ham or shredded beef or a little cooked meat of any kind will do. Or put a few slivers of mild cheese in with the sauce. This will melt while the potatoes are warming.

To add to the attractiveness of a creamed dish, you might set the saucepan under the flame in the grill. Leave the pan under the flame for a few minutes until the top of the sauce is delicately browned and serve immediately.

CROQUETTES

Using a creamed dish for a basis, you can very easily make the more elaborate left over dish called croquettes. Make the cream sauce a little thicker than usual by using two tablespoons of flour to one of butter. Then, add to it the base ingredients (shredded cooked fish, chopped cooked meat or minced ham) and form the mixture into small balls or into flat ovals. Refrigerate for 2 to 3 hours. Finally dip each ball into beaten egg, then into bread crumbs and fry as you would fritters. Serve with tomato sauce or with a hot tartar sauce.

LIGHT DESSERTS FOR LUNCH

These may be as simple as you like: canned fruit of any kind (first cooled in the refrigerator); sliced bananas or peaches with powdered sugar on them; stuffed dates; cake; candy or fruit sauce with cookies. Here is how to make them:

ORANGES AND GRAPEFRUIT

Prepare the orange and the grapefruit in the same way. First cut inside of each compartment with a sharp knife to separate the pulp from the skin. Then, with a pair of scissors, snip off the rays of the white fibrous center. Cut underneath the center and remove it. Fill its place with sugar.

STUFFED DATES

To stuff dates, have ready a saucer of granulated sugar. Crack and shell some nuts. English walnuts, pecans and peanuts are all good for this purpose. Then take out the stones of the dates and fill each date with a piece of nut. Roll the date in sugar until it is no longer sticky.

PRUNES

Prunes, when well prepared, are both rich and delicious. They must be soft and sweet and have a heavy syrup. They should be served cold. Soak prunes overnight in cold water

56.

and in the morning pour off most of the water (leaving about a cupful). Add half a teaspoon of either brown or granulated sugar for each prune. Cover the pan and place in a slow oven. Let the prunes bake for about an hour, adding more water if necessary and keeping the water level the same. Cool before serving.

APPLE SAUCE

Apple sauce is quickly made with a minimum of trouble. Pare five or six good sized cooking apples and cut them into small pieces (throw away all cores and imperfect parts). Barely cover them with cold water in a saucepan. Cover the pan, and simmer for fifteen to twenty minutes or until the apples are soft when tested with a spoon. Drain them in a colander and return to the saucepan. Mash them and add two tablespoons of granulated sugar. Add a pinch of cinnamon. Stir until the sugar is melted. Pour out into a glass dish or into individual dishes to cool.

STRAWBERRY SAUCE

Strawberry sauce (not quite so elaborate as strawberry preserves) is made just as apple sauce is made except that very little water is used. To a pint of berries, add only one half cup of water. Cook until they are soft. Drain them, mash them and add granulated sugar to taste with a drop or two of lemon juice.

57.

DINNER

DINNER

A perfect dinner satisfies but does not stuff you. It is pleasant to eat because it is made up of a number of surprising and delicious things, each one of which leaves you wishing for just a bite or two more. In the end the composite effect is very satisfying. In planning the meal, the great point is to have it balanced. That is, the courses should dovetail into one another without repetitions of the same food element. No one course should be too heavy in itself. A meal of cream of potato soup, roast pork, sweet potatoes, coleslaw and blanc-mange, for instance, would be poorly chosen for two reasons: it repeats the potato element by having potatoes both in the soup and in the main course. Also, the pork dish is much too heavy to follow a heavy soup. If this meal were changed to a thin soup, roast pork, sweet potatoes, a plain lettuce salad with French dressing and blanc–mange, it would be balanced.

In general, with roasts of meat, steaks, and braised meat dishes, a thin light soup or boullion is preferable and the salad and dessert courses should be light. By a light dessert is meant one not using much milk, eggs, or flour in the preparation. Fruit, gelatine, fruit whips, and cottage pudding are light desserts. Pie, custards, puddings and rich cakes are heavy ones.

Make a festival of dinner by always using the finest china, silverware and table coverings you have. Use a low light for the table (a chandelier or a table lamp). Finish the meal with after dinner coffee in little cups.

SOUPS

Perhaps the easiest thing to learn to make well (and certainly the most economical thing) is soup. There are three kinds we will look at: meat soup, vegetable soup, and cream soup.

The theory of soup making is the drawing out of juice from a solid substance. So the soup must be begun with cold water. Hot water would sear the surface of the material and in that way keep in a large proportion of the juices. The process of drawing out juice is a long one. Therefore, the soup must be allowed to cook at a very low temperature for a long time. Since the juices, as they are drawn from the solid substance, must not be lost by going up in steam, the soup kettle needs a tight fitting lid.

Of the three kinds, meat soups are the most important since they have the widest range of variation and are most appropriate for dinner.

You can buy meat or meat bone for soup but scraps of steak, chops, and even gristly, bony parts of roasts will do just as well (and cost nothing). Soup can be made with either cooked or uncooked meat.

You will need a varied stock of seasonings. The following are suggested: thyme, sage, powdered clove, whole cloves, cinnamon, ginger, allspice, celery seed, mace, and some bay leaves. Besides these, onions should be on hand and so should parsley (fresh or dried).

MEAT SOUP

If you have just had a roast of beef or veal and have used every bit of the lean meat, then you have nothing left but the foundation of bone, the fat, and stringy meat. Put all this in the soup kettle, salt it freely as you would salt that much meat at the table, and add to it half a teaspoon of any liquid used to give flavor and a brillant brown color to soups and gravies (like boullion , etc.). Add half a bay leaf, a slice of onion, three cloves and just enough water to cover it. Put the lid on tight and set the kettle over a low fire.

Start the soup in the morning if possible. Let it simmer all day until bedtime. Add more water during the day if necessary to keep about the original quantity. You will not have to stay at home to watch the soup, for it cannot go dry if the lid is on tight and the fire very low. After it has cooked, strain it through a wire colander to remove from it all solid matter and let the liquid stand overnight in a cool place. In the morning it will be covered with a thin cake of white fat. Lift this off, carefully, and save it for cooking purposes. Soup fat is always savory from the seasonings. The soup, if it has stood in the refrigerator all night, will probably be in the form of gelatin (an infallible sign of good soup).

Whether it has gelatinized or not, it may be thinned a little, like canned soup, before being heated up for serving. During the reheating, you might cook a tablespoon of rice in the soup or a stalk or two of celery cut into dice. There are many brands of noodles on the market that are made particularly for soup. They may be cooked in about ten minutes. If there is more soup than can be used at one meal, the rest will last for two or three days in the refrigerator. You can change the character of it, on the second reheating, by adding a spoon of tomato sauce to it.

You can use two or more kinds of meat in the same soup and both cooked and uncooked meat. The seasonings may be varied to suit your taste. Use only a little of each seasoning (particularly bay leaf) and try to have one flavor more dominant in the soup just described. Cabbage might have been used instead of celery (only two leaves of it) and a pinch of mace instead of bay leaf, or a teaspoon of dried parsley instead of cloves. You should experiment.

VEGETABLE SOUP

The vegetable soups, commonly called purees, are thick and very nourishing. They may be made in an hour or less. Potatoes, cooked dried beans or peas, and canned vegetables of all kinds are used for a foundation.

They follow the principle of meat soups. Cut the vegetables into small pieces, salt and add seasoning. This may be a slice of onion, some celery tops, a pinch of dry mustard. Cover with cold water, put a lid on the kettle, and cook over a slow fire. At the end of an hour, hold a wire colander over a bowl and strain the soup into the bowl. With a potato masher, force the vegetables through the colander. You must keep clearing the under part of the colander with a tablespoon as the vegetable pulp comes through. When this is done, melt a tablespoon of butter in the empty saucepan, add to it a tablespoon of flour and stir until they are smooth. Gradually add the soup mixture, with the saucepan over the fire, stirring as you pour. Let the whole thing come to a boil. It will be thick and well blended. It is now ready to be served or to be set away to be reheated and served later.

CREAM SOUP

Cream soups are more expensive than the others, a little more complicated in the making, and too rich to serve with any but a very light dinner (or as the main dish for lunch).

They are made in the top part of a double boiler. Almost any vegetable except dried ones that require long cooking may be used. Even dried ones may be used if they have first been cooked soft. Celery, corn, string beans, carrots, lettuce, and asparagus are most often used.

For an example, choose cream of celery soup. Use only the rough, outer stalks, saving the tender ones for an hors d'oeuvre at lunch. Wash the stalks and leaves, scrape away any brown places and cut the celery into small pieces. Put these, with all the leaves, in the double boiler. Salt them, add half an onion cut into slices and half a carrot cut into thin threads. Pour over this a pint of milk or half a pint each of milk and water. Put boiling water in the bottom of the double boiler and set the soup on over a high flame until the water is boiling rapidly in the lower pan. Then turn the fire down rather low (just enough to keep the water at the boiling point). Let the soup cook, tightly covered, for three quarters of an hour. At the end of this time, strain it through a wire colander and then carefully take out the pieces of celery and carrot. Add them to the liquid. In the saucepan, mix butter and flour and add the soup to them gradually as you did when making the puree. Be sure not to let the soup reach the boiling point for it is likely to curdle if it boils. It may be reheated without the double boiler, but must never boil.

COOKING FATS

You will find it convenient to keep the fat that you skim off meat soups. Store them separate from the fat drained from bacon or ham (for both types of fat have their special uses). Soup fat may be used for all meat frying, for frying fritters, batter cakes and croquettes. It can also be used for dumplings to go with a meat stew or for pie crust of a salmon pie. Bacon and ham fat may be substituted for butter in frying eggs (including omelet and scrambled eggs) and potatoes. Tomatoes are much improved in flavor if they are fried in bacon rather than butter.

The choice of appropriate fats for each kind of cooking lies with your own tastes and with the demands of economy. Butter might be used for every kind of cooking or baking. Butter, however, is very expensive. Margarine is an excellent substitute. Olive oil, which is excellent for frying steaks or reheating green or canned vegetables, also is expensive. Lard's uses are limited almost exclusively to pastry making and to the frying of batter cakes, fritters, and breaded meats (when the cheaper and more savory soup fat is lacking. A reliable, moderately economical fat which can be used for virtually every purpose except for the making of cream sauces or for frying eggs, is shortening. It comes in cans of various sizes, fitted with detachable lids, is mild in flavor and as white as lard. This manufactured cooking fat can safely be used instead of butter in any kind of baking. In the baking of white cakes, particularly, it is superior to the butter because of its lack of color.

MEAT

There is no absolute way to cook any cut of meat. Personal taste enters into consideration and so does the amount of time and money you have to spend. If you are interested in creating meat dishes that will be remembered for their new flavor or delicious sauce and garnish, you should cook the same cut of meat differently every time you have it.

Even if you do not want to be creative, you will at least want to avoid bleakness in your meat cooking. Examples of poor dishes are: pale and stringy boiled beef served with only its own thin liquid to give it zest; steak that always tastes the same along with a uniformly mild typical gravy; ungarnished, bedraggled looking baked meat and stews that never vary their carrots, potatoes and lamb.

If you once understand the principle upon which all meat is cooked, you can form your own theories and you will find that the cooking of meat becomes a fascinating never solved game. Meat, to be made appetizing, must undergo two processes. It must first be browned to keep its flavor and juices. Then it must be cooked long enough to soften its fibers. The browning is done on top of the stove and usually in the pan in which the meat is to be cooked tender. The cooking is done in the oven, under the grill of the oven, or on top of the stove (according to the nature and size of the cut).

The meat is seasoned during the second process rather than the first because salt is apt to make the juices run out. Since it is the seasoning, even more than the cooking, that makes the meat good, you can see how important it is to sur-

67.

round the meat during the period of softening with savory elements for it to absorb. If the piece of meat is not one of the tender cuts, such as tenderloin steak (also lamb chops, sirloin or porterhouse steak and veal liver), or if it is chunky in shape and therefore suitable mostly for roasting or baking, then its surrounding element should be liquid. Otherwise the surrounding element may be sliced vegetables, herbs, or a dash of condiment.

So we get the general rule: tender, thin cuts of meat, including tender steaks and chops, are cooked quickly without any surrounding liquid. They are either fried or broiled. They are made savory with dry seasoning, not added, sometimes, until the process of cooking is finished. The seasonings are then often put into the sauce that is served with the meat. On the other hand, the bigger pieces of meat, such as three or four pound roasts and broiling cuts, and the pieces that come from the muscular parts of the animals (flank steaks, rump steaks, shoulder, and shank) are cooked in liquid for a long time. Then, in most cases, this liquid forms the basis for the sauce to be eaten with the meat.

STEAK

Because the process is shorter, you might begin with steak cooking. The steak, however, is an expensive cut and having learned how to cook it, you will be wise to keep it only for special occasions. Concentrate, then, on the more slowly cooked meats for economy.

Oil a heavy skillet with butter, margarine or olive oil. When the skillet is hot, drop in the steak and brown both sides quickly. Browning helps seal in juices and flavor. It is also more attractive than a dull grayish looking piece of meat.

68.

If steak is thin, continue cooking on top of the stove. If steak is thick, place it under a preheated broiler 3 inches from the flame. Cook 5 to 10 minutes or until done to suit you.

To flavor steak, try any of the following:

★ An hour before cooking, rub with olive oil and crushed garlic.

★ Take a tablespoon of crushed peppercorns and sprinkle them across the steak, pressing them into the meat with the palm of your hand.

★ Just before cooking, cut slivers of garlic and stick several into little slits in the meat.

★Pan juices poured over the cooked steak are a nice touch. If there is not enough to use, add 1 or 2 tablespoons of water or wine to the pan. Heat and stir. Add seasonings and serve.

CHOPS AND LIVER

Lamb chops are cooked just like steak. Pork and veal chops (veal simply means the meat of a young calf) need a little longer period after they are browned. Consequently, lamb chops may be broiled because they are as tender as steak but it is safer to fry pork and veal chops.

Turn the flame down very low and let the pork and veal chops simmer with a lid on the pan for fifteen or twenty minutes. Veal liver is treated like pork and veal chops but must have a preliminary coating over it to hold in the juices even before it is put in the pan to brown. The coating is put on with boiling water. Put the liver in a colander and pour the boiling water over it until the surfaces get white. Cook liver just like pork chops, allowing it to simmer after it is brown.

EASY ROAST BEEF

Meat cooks better if brought to room temperature first. Unfortunately, this is not always possible so keep an eye on your roast and check it occasionally for degree of doneness.

It takes twenty minutes per pound to cook a medium rare roast containing bone. For a rolled roast or other roast without bone, you will need about 30 minutes per pound.

Wipe meat before cooking and sear or brown. This can be done on top of the stove in a heavy, preheated pan just as you sear steak. It can also be done in the oven by preheating the oven to 550 degrees and reducing heat to 350 degrees as soon as the meat is placed in the oven.

If meat is lean, baste it with pan drippings. Basting is simply taking the juices surrounding the roast and pouring them over the roast while it is cooking. This is to prevent the roast from drying out while cooking. Baste about every 15 minutes. A roast can be flavored the same as a steak. Also follow steak instructions for gravy. If you want to salt meat, allow about 1 teaspoon per pound. However, salt will allow the juices to escape during cooking so be careful.

TRADITIONAL ROAST BEEF

If you want a roast of beef, try a three pound piece from the rump instead of buying the more expensive rib roast. You will find the flavor excellent and there will be more meat left over for the next day. This is a very lean, meaty cut. A rib roast has all the waste of the rib bones. The rump roast is also called a rolled rump or a standing rump.

Here is one way to cook it: In a baking pan which has a tight fitting lid, melt two tablespoons of butter (use the stove top with a medium fire). Drop into this two medium sized onions, pared and sliced. Salt them and stir them until they are pale brown and beginning to soften. Then push them to one side of the pan. Lay the piece of meat in. Hold each surface of it against the bottom of the pan until it is seared all over and brown. Then season it with salt and pepper and a pinch of mace. Take it out of the pan. Add a tablespoon of flour to the grease in the pan, stir it, and let it get brown and blended. Mix the onions with the flour and add two cups of cold water, slowly, stirring all the time. When this sauce has reached the boiling point, put the meat back in the pan, turn out the fire under it, cover the pan tightly and put it in a 550 degree oven. As soon as the pan is in the oven, turn the flame down to 350 degrees. Let the meat bake for about two hours. Look at it once or twice in that time to see if there is enough water in the pan. If you like, you can cook potatoes in with the meat. This will give them a savory meat taste and brown them too. Pare the potatoes and cut them into quarters. The more finely cut they are, the less time they will need to cook. Lay them beside the meat and turn the oven fire up higher. They will be done in twenty to twenty-five minutes.

Then the meat and potatoes are ready to go on their platter. The sauce is ready too. It will be brown, smooth, and savory of onions.

POT ROAST

This way of baking meat is scarcely different from oven roasting except that a pot roast is cooked entirely on top of the stove. So, if it is a pot roast you want, proceed just as before but allow the baking pan to simmer over a slow burner for about three hours. Instead of putting potatoes in with it, you

could make macaroni or rice. Both of these will need the richness of taste that meat juice can give them. Put them in an
hour before the meat is done.

BAKED MEATS

This is for some of the flatter baking pieces such as: round
or flank steak, double pork chops or breaded chops. You follow the same principle of browning the meat first in a frying
or baking pan and then making a sauce to bake the meat in or
simply putting water or soup stock in the pan instead. Of
course, the smaller and flatter the piece of meat is, the less
water is necessary and the less time is needed to cook the
meat tender. As a rule, add just enough liquid to come halfway up the bulk of the meat.

Baked steak and stuffed or breaded chops need some special preparation before they are ready to be browned in the
pan and baked.

Steak is often breaded or stuffed before being baked. To
bread it, cut into rounds just as you would cut sirloin or tenderloin steak into rounds for frying, and remove most of the
fat. Beat an egg in a bowl; season it with salt and pepper. Put
some bread or cracker crumbs in a shallow dish. Dip each
piece of steak first into the egg, then into the crumbs. Finish
by putting it in the hot frying pan. Veal chops, pork chops,
and mutton chops are breaded the same way.

To stuff a steak, like flank steak, rub it thoroughly with a
damp piece of paper, lay it out, whole, on a floured board and
sprinkle it with crumbled bits of bread with butter. Then roll
the steak up like a jelly roll, tie it with string, and put it in the
frying pan. Sear it well. Add water and seasoning. Bake at 325
degrees for 1½ hours.

72.

Either lamb or pork chops may be bought double, with a pocket cut between the two to hold a stuffing. Lamb chops are so small that they may be fried, slowly, when they are stuffed (instead of being baked). It is safer, however, to bake them. Bake for half an hour to three quarters of an hour in a moderate oven. Make the stuffing of crumbled bread, seasoned with leaf sage and salt and pepper. With lamb chops, you can get a delicate flavor if you moisten the stuffing with a teaspoon of tomato sauce.

Experiment with your stuffed pork chops and lamb chops by baking them without a lid over the baking pan and without any liquid added to them. Use more grease in the browning of them. As they bake, occasionally lift up some of the grease in the bottom of the pan with a spoon and pour it over them. They should get crisp on the outside and mealy inside.

This process is real roasting. It is suitable for all fat roasts, such as roasts of veal, pork, or lamb. It is not best for beef roasts, unless it is very skillfully done.

It has the advantage of making the roast drier inside than baking makes it. Also of getting the outside crisper and keeping from the meat all extraneous flavors, which seasoned sauce or hot water will give to it.

This plain roasting may be varied by roasting with the help of sliced vegetables. Season these and lay the roasting meat on top of them after you have browned it in another pan. As the meat roasts, the vegetable liquid will mix with the grease from the meat itself, so that what you will have to baste the roast with will be its own very savory gravy. To roast, have the fire high for about twenty minutes, then turn it to a moderate height for the rest of the cooking. The meat is done when you can pick little shreds from it easily with a fork.

MEAT LOAF

Meat loaf is economical and depends for its flavor upon the seasoning it gets. Ground meat is at best almost flavorless. The loaf should be held together with egg. Beat up one egg for each pound of ground beef. Season the egg with salt and pepper and add the meat. Then mix in half a cup of bread crumbs to increase the bulk. Cooked rice or mashed potatoes will do even better if they are on hand. Make the meat into a flat loaf and, when it is compact, lay it in a casserole dish with a lid. Cook in the oven at 350°. When the under side of the loaf is brown, turn it over to brown the upper side. Lift it with a spatula. Be careful so the loaf does not break. You can cook an onion (sliced) in the grease around the meat. Use this to form the foundation for a piquant sauce. Instead of an onion, a sliced tomato or a quarter of a can of stewed tomatos can be used. You could also sprinkle flour on top of the meat loaf and rub some flour with a spoon into the grease in the pan (this way there will be a gravy around the meat when it is done). Drop some Worcestershire sauce or catsup into this before serving it over the loaf.

STEW

Buy three pounds or more of lean stew meat cut in cubes. Drop these, after you have floured them, into the frying pan and be sure to brown every side of every piece. Stewed meat is cooked entirely under water. So, after browning the pieces, pour over them enough boiling water (or soup if you have it) to cover the meat. Put the lid on the pan, turn the flame down to simmering heat, and let the stew cook for an hour or more. Then add any vegetables you want: sweet potatoes will go well with veal or lamb; rice or Irish potatoes with beef; add carrots, cooked or canned lima beans, asparagus, string beans, peas, or celery. Cook stew a half hour longer if you have potatoes so they will soften (potatoes, of course, should be cut up fine).

Then, in a small mixing bowl, make dumplings to finish and thicken the stew. Sift a teaspoon of baking powder with a cup of flour and a pinch of salt. Mix with the flour a teaspoon of butter until the two are blended. Do this mixing with your fingers. Then add just enough cold water (not more than a quarter of a cup) to make the flour into a soft wad. Drop this, a tablespoon at a time, into the stew. Cover tightly and cook for fifteen minutes. The stew and dumplings are now ready to be served.

CASSEROLE DISHES

Based on the principle of the stew (that is: cut the meat into pieces, brown them, and cook them for a long time in a covering liquid) is the theory of casserole baking. It is the favorite cooking method of a lot of people. Casseroles can be cooked either on top of the stove or in the oven. This is a good plan because it makes it possible to do the browning and cooking the the same pan. This conserves the flavor and utilizes all of the juice.

For casserole cooking, you can use any kind of meat (cooked or uncooked) with almost any kind of sauce or vegetables. Make sure the seasoning is adequate. The meat must cook long enough to be thoroughly tender. The vegetables must be adapted to one another in both color and taste. Carrots and sweet potatoes, for instance, would not be good in combination because they are the same color. Carrots would go well, however, with peas or lima beans or string beans. Celery is almost tasteless (although it smells good when it is cooked) so it should be put with canned corn or beets or tomatoes.

Here is a suggestion for a casserole dish: In a frying pan, melt a tablespoon of butter, and brown in it a quarter pound of ground beef and two sliced onions. Place these in a greased casserole, season them with salt, pepper, a pinch of mace and a pinch of powdered clove. Finally, add pared and diced potatoes. Pour in half a can of tomatoes. The tomato liquid should come to the top of the potatoes. If necessary, add enough cold water to fill out. On the very top, put a tablespoon of uncooked rice. Season the rice. Cover the casserole and bake for 1¼ hours in a 400 degree oven. It is done when the rice is crisp and brown. Serve in the casserole. If you use one of the enameled casseroles, do the premiminary browning in it too.

Even small amounts of meat may be made into casserole dishes by adding vegetables and cooking in a sauce. If you have a small piece of round or sirloin steak left from another meal (cooked or uncooked), you can combine it with a quarter of a can of tomatoes, a quarter of a can of corn and a potato sliced thin. Bake until the potato is soft. If the steak is uncooked, brown all of its surfaces before adding it to the casserole.

HOW MUCH MEAT TO BUY

● A sirloin steak weighing about a pound and a half will serve four persons.

● A porterhouse steak will serve two or three.

● It is a good estimate to allow two chops for each person or one double chop.

● One pound of liver will serve four persons.

● A meat loaf made from one pound of meat will serve three.

● A three or four pound piece of meat (baked or in a pot roast) will serve about six persons.

● One pound of stewing meat will hardly do for more than two persons because of the amount of waste in bone and fat. Three and one half pounds is a good amount to serve 6 to 8 people.

● In buying veal steak, or round steak, allow one pound for two.

HINTS ABOUT MEAT

WARMING ROAST: Instead of warming roast beef over in gravy, try putting it on a small tin pie plate and placing it in a steamer over boiling water. In about half an hour you have a fresh juicy roast. When warming over small bits of meat, this same method may be used. You can add some finely chopped onion, a dash of Worchestershire sauce or a little mixed mustard to improve the flavor.

BAKING HAM: To bake a ham so that it will retain all of its flavor, encase it with a paste made of common flour and water. Make sure that the steam cannot escape. Bake in a hot oven (450 degrees) and allow a quarter of an hour for every pound. When cooked, the paste can be easily removed and it takes all the rind with it.

BRAISING MEAT: Braising is steaming meats in their own juices, a method suitable for solid pieces of meat not tender enough for roasting but of better quality than those used for soups or stews.

SALTING MEAT: Never salt meat until it is ready to be served. If salted before cooking, it will toughen the meat and tend to extract the juices.

SAVE GRAVY: Save the leftover gravy from the roast. It comes in very handy when the roast has been reduced to stew or hash. You can use this gravy instead of water when making stew or hash.

CLOVES IN STEW: Put a clove into the Irish stew for a savory flavor and a sprig of parsley into a pea soup or a dish of peas.

MEAT TENDERIZER: A little vinegar cooked with coarse meat helps to make it tender. You could also dip the meat into vinegar before cooking.

CARVING MEATS: In carving a rolled roast of beef, cut thin slices in a horizontal direction across the surface of the meat.

If you have a porterhouse steak, place it on the platter with the broad end of the steak to the right of the carver. It is much more convenient if the knife is smaller and narrower than the regulation carving knife used for roasts. If you can easily do it, it is a good idea to remove the bone in the center of the steak. When this is done, you can cut the steak into narrow slices and don't have to hack at it.

A fillet of beef, on the other hand, is cut into thick slices. You run your fork down into the meat at the first joint above the end of the round bone to the left. Beginning at the top of the central portion of the roast, cut in slices down to the bone until the large bone at the right is reached. Then turn the knife and run it along the bone to loosen the slices.

In carving a boiled or roast ham, the small knuckle is placed to the right of the carver. Cut thin slices straight to the knuckle, inserting the knife at the top of the ham.

A crown of lamb or pork is very easy to carve because the roast is cut at the butchers. All that has to be done is to cut the ribs apart. One rib is a portion. This is usually served with some of the vegetables that are put in the crown when it is brought to the table.

SAUCES

It is obvious that in the cooking and serving of meat, you are limited in variety only by the number of sauces you can invent. Take, for instance, the serving of a veal cutlet. It can have a tomato sauce one day, a velvet sauce the next day, a brown sauce the next, then an onion sauce, then a cheese sauce and so on. The difference in the taste of the cutlet will be surprising. The same is true of the serving of fish and vegetables.

It is important, then, to understand the formation of sauces.

Basically, the foundation of a sauce is the juice extracted from meat, fish, or vegetables (separately or in combination). This sauce may be gotten by putting soup in the juice instead of water. You can also cook sliced vegetables and herbs in butter for a short time to extract their juices. You can also squeeze the juices from uncooked fruits and vegetables. Of course, there are commercial bouillon cubes, canned stock and liquids used in preparing vegetables which are all good sources for the sauce juice.

A sauce is usually thickened a little. This is done by first mixing flour with butter or other grease that has been melted in a frying pan. Then add the liquid element slowly, stirring all the time, over a low flame.

The color of the sauce will depend in large measure upon the way you prepare the thickening. If you leave the flour in the grease long enough to brown it, the sauce will be brown. If you add the liquid immediately after the flour is blended, the sauce will be white. Of course, a dark soup stock added to the sauce will make it dark in any case. There are also a number of commercial items which will add a brown color and meaty taste to your sauce.

In order to have materials on hand for saucemaking, you will have to preserve every speck of food that has flavor in it. When you find half wilted pieces of celery on a stalk, cut them up and cook them or juice them. If you cook them, cook them for an hour or so in salted water. The resulting cooked juice, when strained, will make a delicious sauce for that evening's meat course. Use it instead of plain water. Cabbage leaves may be treated in the same way and so may any vegetables. Radishes cooked for two hours or less will get soft enough to be pushed through a wire strainer if you do not have a juicer. Season them with a dash of salt, pepper and dry mustard. This semi–liquid, you will discover, is a great sauce for halibut or fried oysters.

Before washing a baking pan, put a little cold water in it and with a spoon or a fork you can scrape down from the sides all the brown particles. Let these come to a boil with the cold water. Season the liquid and set it away to form the liquid part of your next dinner sauce.

Here are some representative sauces:

PAN GRAVY SAUCE

If you are having stuffed pork chops, bake them with a little hot water around them . Remove the chops from the baking pan when finished and put the pan over a fire. It will have in it a mixture of grease and meat stock. With a tablespoon, lift off most of the grease, leaving the browned stock in the pan. Put the grease you lifted off in a small bowl. Blend the grease with a tablespoon of flour. Pour a spoonful of liquid from the pan into the bowl. When the thickening is smooth, add it to the pan liquid. Then pour on enough soup stock or cold water to make as much sauce as you need. Season it with salt and pepper. When it is thick and boiling, it is ready to serve.

If you find that the water has all boiled away, or if you roast the stuffed chops instead of baking them, simply add one half cup cold water to the grease in the pan and set it over a hot fire. Season it and bring to a boil. Stir vigorously to include in the sauce all particles of browned fat.

TARTAR SAUCE

Tartar sauce may be served hot or cold. It is made of one half cup cream sauce and one half cup mayonnaise. Add to this a pinch of mustard, a sweet pickle cut fine and either three stuffed olives (chopped fine) or a teaspoon of chopped capers. Serve tartar sauce with left over meat or with fish of any kind.

BUTTER SAUCE

Suppose you are having broiled steak and want a new sort of sauce to pour over it. In this case, you will not have any residue of grease or liquid to use as a foundation for the sauce. You will have to manufacture the whole thing. Put a tablespoon of butter in a pan. Cut a small carrot into shreds, break up a branch of parsley, and season these with sage. Let them fry gently in the butter for a minute. Then pour in two tablespoons of milk and cover the pan. After they have simmered for ten minutes, strain the resulting liquid through a wire colander. Cream half a tablespoon of flour in a cup with half a tablespoon of butter. Then moisten with a little of the vegetable liquid. Next, add the thickening to the rest of the liquid. Bring it to the boiling point and serve it over the steak.

BUTTER GARNISH

This is a simple sauce for a steak or fish. Put the hot meat or fish on a hot platter. Drop on each piece some unmelted butter which you have seasoned in a bowl with salt and a teaspoon of either lemon juice or vinegar. The hot meat will melt the butter. Garnish this sauce, after it is on the platter, with chopped parsley or sliced celery stalks.

BUTTER ORANGE SAUCE

Another butter sauce is made by melting the butter in a saucepan, adding to it the juice of half an orange, salt, pepper and paprika. Then beat it with a fork until it is foamy. Pour it over the meat.

VELVET SAUCE

Velvet sauce is very nourishing. It uses the yolk of an egg in its preparation and is very good to serve with warmed up white meat, such as veal, pork, lamb, or chicken. To make this sauce, melt a tablespoon of grease in a pan. Blend a tablespoon of flour with it just long enough to make the mixture smooth. Add a cup of either milk or water (cold). Stir this until the sauce is beginning to thicken, then set it off the fire. Beat an egg yolk in a bowl with a teaspoon of cold water (added to make the egg blend easily). Season the egg. Add to it a little of the hot sauce, stirring vigorously.

Then pour the egg mixture into the remaining sauce. Put the saucepan over the fire again but be sure to take it off before the sauce boils (or it will curdle).

CHEESE SAUCE

A cheese sauce is made with the same foundation as velvet sauce. It uses butter, flour and milk (water cannot be used). After the sauce is beginning to thicken, add half a cup of grated cheese to it and turn the flame down low. The sauce is done when the cheese has melted. This sauce is thick and rich. It is particularly fine to serve over an omelet or with a slice of halibut steak.

VINAIGRETTE SAUCE

Vinaigrette sauce goes well with roast beef, fried fish or breaded meat. Warm in a pan one tablespoon of vinegar, two tablespoons of olive oil, salt, pepper and the following ingredients chopped fine: one onion, a slice of cabbage, a sprig of parsley and a sweet pickle. Pour this over the meat or fish.

SIMPLE SAUCE

A simple sauce is made by adding a very little flour to the juices, half a teaspoon is a safe amount, stirring this until it is brown and blended. Then slowly add less than a cupful of cold water or cold left over soup if you have it. Stir constantly and season with salt and pepper. When this is smooth, it is ready to be poured over the steak.

FISH

Fish is already very tender when it is bought. Consequently, the cooking is never a long process. Because fish is one of the most common sources of ptomaine poisoning, the greatest care must be used in its selection and cleaning. Fresh fish have bright red gills, clear, open eyes, firm flesh (not flabby) and firm scales. If the scales are dull and come off easily, do not buy the fish. Frozen fish are put into the freezers fresh and are frozen so quickly that there is no chance of decomposition. Thaw fish by putting them in cold water until all the frost is removed, then cook them as fresh fish.

Fresh fish may be fried, baked, broiled or stuffed (just like meat). It is low in calories, quick cooking and a good source of protein. The following recipes use fresh fish or thawed frozen fish.

FRIED FISH

Trout, bass, and perch are all adaptable to frying. Wash them first with cold water and dry them with a paper towel. Salt them inside and out. Dip them in milk, then in flour, and drop into hot fat. Cook them fast until they are browned on both sides. This should take about 8 minutes. Then place them on a hot platter garnished with a stalk of parsley that has cooked for a minute or two in the hot fat. Just before serving, add a teaspoon of tomato sauce on top of each fish.

If you want to fry a larger fish, cut it into several pieces first and use this opportunity to take out the backbone. Cook the same as above.

BAKED FISH

Any fish may be stuffed or baked. Wash it first and dry it. Make a stuffing of crumbled bread, a quarter of a minced onion, salt, and pepper. Lay this along one side of the fish and then squeeze lemon juice over it. Close the other side of the fish down over the stuffing. Tie with a string. Put the fish in a frying pan with a little melted butter and sprinkle flour over the skin. When it is browned in the butter, put a strip of bacon on top of the fish. Add half a cup of boiling water. Put the lid tightly on the pan and bake in a 375 degree oven for half an hour.

Instead of baking the stuffed fish, you might broil it. Set it in the broiler and grill it as you would broil a beefsteak, starting with a hot fire to brown the skin, then lowering the flame to cook the fish through. Broiling will not take more than fifteen minutes.

With baked or broiled fish, a velvet sauce is good. You could also use the simpler one of melted butter with lemon juice.

FISH IN CASSEROLE

If you can get a piece from the small end of a salmon or halibut (weighing about two pounds), you can make a baked casserole dish with a delicious sauce. Melt two tablespoons of butter in a pan and fry in it two small sliced onions. Fry until the onions are soft. Add a cup of tomato soup, let the soup heat, then season the sauce with salt and pepper. Put this in the bottom of a greased casserole. Add the piece of fish (wash and dry the fish first) and cover the casserole. Bake for half an hour in a moderately hot oven. It will be done when the fish falls away from the bone if you touch it with a fork. Serve in the casserole. Pickerel or whitefish may be baked in this same way.

ANOTHER CASSEROLE FISH DISH

A very delicate way to cook either large or small fish is to chop up about a cup of vegetables and herbs (mushrooms, parsley, onions, celery and thyme will do). Then, in a soup kettle or a casserole that can stand on top of the stove, melt a tablespoon of butter. Sprinkle a tablespoon of flour over the butter. Add half of the herbs. Lay on this one or two small fish (wash, dried, and salted) and cover them with a layer of bread crumbs. Put on next the other half of the herbs and add another layer of crumbs. Squeeze over this the juice of one lemon and add a cupful of some liquid (preferably a vegetable or thin soup of meat—otherwise, just use hot water). Cover the pan and cook on top of the stove at a simmering temperature for half an hour. Serve all of this dish using the herbs for a garnishing.

FRIED HALIBUT

Halibut is a easily obtainable fish steak. The quickest way to cook it is to fry it. First dip it in milk. Then in bread crumbs. Use two tablespoons of cooking fat for one slice of halibut. Brown each side in the hot fat, then turn the flame down low. Cover the pan and let the fish cook for twenty minutes. Serve it with tomato or cheese sauce.

BAKED HALIBUT

You may also bake halibut after you have dipped it in milk and bread crumbs. Have more cooking fat in the pan than you would for frying. Cover the baking pan and set it in a 300 degree oven for half an hour. Turn the halibut once during this time to allow both sides to get brown.

BAKED HALIBUT

When tomatoes are in season, try this way of baking halibut: Lay it in a frying pan with melted butter. Season it well with salt and pepper. Then slice tomatoes over top of it. On top of the tomatoes, put about half a cup of shredded green peppers. Season these and bake in a moderately hot oven, with no lid on the pan, until the top of the fish is brown. Serve with a dab of unmelted butter on top of the halibut.

POACHED HALIBUT

Halibut may be poached, if you want to make a very elaborate and decorative dish of it. In a frying pan, melt a tablespoon of butter and onion. Stir in a tablespoon of flour. Blend it with the butter and onion. Add a cup of milk. Season this sauce. Bring it to a boil while stirring it. Then add to it a few thin shreads of carrot. Lay the halibut in the pan. Cover the pan and cook the fish at the simmering point for about twenty-five minutes. Lift the lid occasionally and baste the top of the fish. Lift the slice with a spatula to let the sauce run under it. About five minutes before the halibut is done, light the oven. Then, after the poaching is done, set the pan under the flame of the grill to brown the fish and sauce. Serve it covered with sauce.

SALMON LOAF

Canned or fresh salmon may be made into several quickly cooked dishes. Perhaps the most practical of them is salmon loaf. This is really a form of souffle. To make it, drain a pound can of salmon and separate the fish from the bones and skin. In a greased baking dish that has a rounded bottom, beat two eggs. Salt the eggs. Add the salmon and mash it down to mix it thoroughly with the egg. Add about a quarter cup of milk. Set the baking dish in a moderately hot oven. In twenty minutes or less, the loaf will be done. The top of it will be firm and brown. Have a hot platter ready to receive it. Then, with a blunt knife or spatula, loosen the loaf around the edges and run the knife underneath it. Drop it out upside down on the platter. Pour over it a cream sauce or any piquant sauce you can make from vegetable liquid (such as radish or celery sauce). Be sure not to take the loaf out of the baking dish until it is firm on top.

SALMON PIE

A salmon pie is made by creaming the salmon first (a cup of plain cream sauce to a can of salmon). Put the creamed salmon in the bottom of a greased shallow baking dish. Cover the top with pie crust. Bake in a 450 degree oven until the crust is brown (about ten or fifteen minutes).

BAKED TUNA

A tasty dish is to be made from a can of tuna fish combined with a cup or more of mashed potatoes. Butter a baking dish. Beat an egg and mix the tuna fish with it. Add and mix the mashed potato and half a cup of milk. Put this in the baking dish and bake it without a lid, in a hot oven, until the top is brown. Serve with a hot sauce vinaigrette.

FRIED OYSTERS

Fried oysters are very simple to prepare. Use large sized ones. Drain them. Put them in pairs with the gills at opposite ends. Have a beaten egg in a bowl and a shallow dish of bread or cracker crumbs. Dip each pair of oysters first in egg, then in crumbs and lastly drop it into hot cooking fat. This fat need not be abundant enough to cover the oysters. Use about three tablespoons to a pint of oysters. When the under side of each fried oyster is crisp and brown, turn it. Make sure the oysters are crisp and brown before turning or they will separate. Keep the fire at moderate heat. Do not cover the pan (that would make the oysters soggy). They will fry in ten to fifteen minutes.

Serve with the oysters the following sauce: Drop a little flour into the fat the oysters cooked in. Stir in a tablespoon of catsup. Add the juice of a whole lemon and a half a cup of water. With the flame up high, stir this sauce rapidly and, when it is bubbling, pour it into a sauce boat which will be served at the table.

HOW MUCH FISH TO BUY

● One pound of halibut will serve two persons.

● Allow at least two small fried fish to a serving.

● One pound can of salmon will make a salmon loaf large enough for three persons.

● Use a small can or half of a big one for a salmon pie for two.

● One can of tuna fish will make a baked dish for three.

● Allow three or four fried oysters to a person. One pint will make enough fried oysters for two persons and will leave plenty for oyster soup.

● One pint of milk will make oyster soup for two.

HINTS ABOUT FISH

FISH ODOR: A handful of salt in the dishpan removes the odor of fish from dishes and utensils.

TENDER FISH: Fish cooked in salted acidulated water (lemon or vinegar in water) are sweeter, more tender and hold their shape when removed from the water.

POULTRY

Chickens, turkeys and most birds are reasonably similar in structure so we will discuss the complete cleaning and cooking of a chicken bearing in mind that this is the same for turkeys or other poultry.

First comes the cleaning of the chicken. The dealer will have done this (more or less) thoroughly and will have put back the parts which are edible. You will find, inserting your hand into the opening cut at the tail end, the heart, the liver, the gizzard, and the neck. The first three are called the giblets. The liver will possibly be in one or two pieces (the mutilation of it will be due to the difficulty of removing it from the gall bladder which lies on its under surface). The dealer will have opened the gizzard, taken out the craw, and left the gizzard smoothed out and clean.

With the giblets taken out and the neck removed, it will be easy to look in and see if the lungs and kidneys have been removed. Often these are not touched by the dealer, because they are in rather remote places and because their removal is not absolutely essential. The lungs are found one on each side of the backbone. They cling to the ribs and are easily recognized by their red color. The kidneys are at the end of the backbone, resting in a slight depression.

You will know that the chicken is thoroughly cleaned when you can see no red particles inside. When you are sure of this, let cold water run through it, making an outlet for the water at the neck end, if there is not already one, and run the water until it finally runs out clear.

92.

Next, clean the giblets by cutting away from them any extraneous looking membranes or pieces of fat. Cut through the heart to the center of it and take out a little blood vessel you will find there. Wash the giblets under cold running water.

The chicken is now ready for stuffing, if it is to be roasted.

EASY ROAST CHICKEN

Rinse chicken and dry well. Rub skin all over with butter, margarine or olive oil. Brown in frying pan on top of stove. Season with salt. Add poultry seasoning or pepper to taste and, for color, sprinkle with paprika. Place frying pan with chicken in pre–heated oven at 350 degrees. Cook about 30 minutes per pound. Baste occasionally. Chicken is done when drumstick can be twisted easily. Chicken can be seared in oven by pre–heating it to 450 degrees and reducing it at once to 350 degrees when chicken is placed in oven. A stuffed chicken will take slightly longer to cook.

TRADITIONAL STUFFED ROAST CHICKEN

First pre–heat oven to 450 degrees. Salt chicken well. Then make a stuffing of two cups of crumbled bread, seasoned with salt, pepper and sage. Dampen with just enough milk to hold the mass together. Fill the chicken with the stuffing, putting it in from the tail end, then stick one big piece of bread in the opening (as a plug).

Melt two tablespoons of cooking fat in the roaster, lay the chicken in on its back, sprinkle it lightly with flour and let it brown in the oven for about five minutes (with the lid off the roaster). Turn the chicken several times during this period to expose all the surfaces. Reduce the heat to 350 degrees. Then add three cups of hot water to the pan. Drop in the giblets (cut into inch square pieces), cover the pan, and continue the cooking at 350 degrees until the chicken seems tender when it is touched with a fork. Halfway through the cooking, salt the chicken and giblets. Baste two or three times. Add more hot water if necessary.

An hour or an hour and a half should be an adequate length of time for the roasting of a three pound chicken.

When the chicken is done, get it out on a hot platter and make a milk gravy to serve with it. This is done by dissolving a heaping tablespoon of flour in enough milk to cover it plus a half a cup of milk and stirring until the milk is even in consistency. Add this to the liquid left in the roasting pan. Season this gravy and stir it until it boils. It should also thicken at this point. Leave the giblets in the gravy.

BROILED CHICKEN

Cut the chicken in half, splitting it along the back and through the breast. Follow the directions given for the broiling of steak but have a slower fire and test the flesh with a fork to determine when it is cooked throughly. It will cook in about twenty minutes.

FRIED CHICKEN

To prepare a chicken for frying, you must first cut it into pieces. This will require the sharpest knife you have. For ease in cutting and to get an approximate uniformity in the size of the pieces, it will be best to follow this general plan:

Holding the chicken on its back, take one of the legs in your left hand, while with the knife in your right hand you slash down through the skin close to the body. Do not be afraid of cutting away too much skin from around the leg. Bend the leg back until the bone separating it from the body cracks. Cut between the interstices of the broken bone and remove the leg. In the same way, having turned the chicken around so that the remaining leg is at your left, cut off the other leg. Cut through each leg as near as possible to the joint in the middle, which you can locate by feeling for it. Then you will have the thigh pieces separated from the drumsticks. Cut off each wing next. This will be easy to do, because there is no hard bone to cut through. Then cut off the end of the back, running the knife along just below the ribs. Next separate the rest of the back from the breast by following the ends of the ribs and cutting as far as the collar bone. Lastly, slit the breast down while keeping near to the center bone. The piece of neck that will be found attached to the end of the breast bone may be left on and that piece of breast bone will do for soup making or for stewing. After cutting the chicken up, wash every piece in running water.

If it is a young frying chicken (weighing scarcely more than a pound), it is ready to be fried immediately. Roll each piece in flour and drop into a frying pan in which three or four tablespoons of cooking fat are sizzling. 'Brown the pieces over a quick fire, until they are the same color all over. Then put a lid on the pan, turn the flame down, and continue the cooking for five or ten minutes (or until the chicken is tender).

If the chicken is a good sized one, it will need parboiling before it can be fried until tender. Put the pieces in a soup kettle with salt, pepper and not quite enough cold water to cover them. Bring the water slowly to a boil, with the kettle covered, then simmer for as long as is necessary to get the chicken tender. Ten or fifteen minutes will do for a young fowl, but an older one may require an hour's time. Test the degree of tenderness, from time to time, by lifting up bits of the flesh with a fork. When the chicken is tender, take the pieces out of the water, pat dry with paper towels, roll them in flour, and fry them fast. They will not need to cook in the frying pan after they are brown.

BRAISED CHICKEN

Instead of parboiling the chicken first, you may try the following: roll it in flour and put it in a baking pan which has been greased. Cover it with about four cups of water, put a lid on the baking pan, and allow the chicken to bake at a rather low heat for two hours. Canned soup plus water can be used instead of all water. Fry the chicken when it is tender.

CHICKEN FRICASSEE

This is a variation of braised chicken, cooked in a casserole. Parboil the chicken, allowing it to remain only a short time in the water (half an hour should be long enough even for a four pound chicken). Then brown the pieces in hot fat and pack them into a deep casserole. Add a tablespoon of flour to the grease left in the frying pan. Blend the grease and flour until the flour is brown. Then add slowly a pint of milk. Stir until the milk begins to thicken. Pour this sauce over the chicken. Season with celery salt and pepper. Add half a can of mushrooms cut into halves, a green pepper shredded, a piece of pimiento cut fine, and two medium sized sweet potatoes run through the meat grinder. Cover the casserole and bake the chicken in a moderately hot oven until it is tender (about two hours).

CHICKEN POT PIE

For a pot pie, choose a two and a half pound chicken. Cut it up, brown the pieces quickly in hot fat, then put them in a stewing pan with enough boiling water to come half way up the bulk. Cover the pan and simmer until tender. About twenty minutes before it is done, add seasoning, two or three potatoes cut into quarters, and a few new onions cut in half. Cook for ten minutes and then add dumplings (see recipe for dumplings). Serve in fifteen minutes. The whole process of cooking will take from one to two hours.

CHICKEN BROTH

Let the water in which the pieces of chicken were parboiled for frying or fricasseeing go on simmering for an hour or two after the chicken has been taken out of it. Leave the giblets in, the neck, and any other pieces (the wings, for example) which are not very meaty. Allow the broth to stand overnight so that you can remove the fat from it (see chapter on soups). After taking the fat off, the next day, warm it up with two tablespoons of rice (as the rice cooks, it will help thicken the broth). Pick the meat from the wings and add that to the broth.

CHICKEN SALAD

This is an appetizing and attractive way to serve left over chicken. Cut it from the bones, removing skin and gristle, and dice the meat. Add celery cut into small pieces, sweet pickle, pimiento, green peppers shredded or whatever you have on hand that seems appropriate. Put the salad together with mayonnaise. Serve on lettuce or in sandwiches.

TURKEY, DUCK AND GOOSE

Turkey, duck and goose may be cleaned just like chicken and cooked the same too. In stuffing them for roasting, however, it will be found necessary to sew up open places through which the stuffing was put. In stuffing goose, include one onion, cut up fine, with the bread crumbs. Duck needs a hot fire during the whole process of roasting. If it is a young duck, it will roast in from three quarters of an hour to an hour. Goose will require one and a half to three hours. Turkey needs about two and a half hours.

HOW MUCH POULTRY TO BUY

● For seven or eight persons, a roast turkey weighing about eleven pounds will be enough. For the same number of persons, two roast ducks or a large goose will be needed.

● One roast chicken weighing about three pounds will serve three or four.

● One chicken weighing two and a half pounds will make enough salad for four.

● For fried chicken for three people you will need a chicken weighing about two and one half pounds.

● Fricasseed chicken in casserole may be made to serve as many as six or as few as two according to the quantity of other ingredients you put in to cook with it. Where there is a four pound chicken, it is good plan to fricassee half of it, for two or three persons, then to use the rest for salad or creamed on toast.

● In general, a chicken weighing under two pounds will serve only two.

99.

HINTS ABOUT POULTRY

CUTTING CHICKEN: Never chop chicken, meat or celery with a regular meat chopper. Cut them as fine as you desire with a small sharp knife. Chopping is apt to make the article stringy.

BASTING CHICKEN: When basting chicken or any other fowl, do not swing the oven door wide open while basting. Open the door part way, cover your hand with a towel, baste quickly and shut the door so as to keep the heat and steam in the oven.

ROASTING CHICKEN: It is often difficult to remove a tender roast chicken from the pan. Try placing a pancake turner under the chicken and, with the help of a fork in the other hand, lift it out of the roaster without the meat falling to pieces.

100.

POTATOES, RICE AND MACARONI

If you treat potatoes, in your cooking of them, as if they were a rare vegetable; if you are continually in search of strange new ways to fix them; and if you serve just a little of them at a time (rather than a big tureenful), you will find that you can make them the most interesting item of a meal. The same is true for your other starch dishes such as rice and macaroni.

STEAMED POTATOES

By far the best way to cook them is to steam them in a double boiler. For this they should be cut into quarters, without being pared. Put them into the boiler without liquid, salted, and with each piece of potato dotted with butter. They should be soft in three quarters of an hour. Cooked this way, they will be flaky and perfectly seasoned. They may be served just as they are, with the skins removed before they are put on the table, or they may be skinned and mashed with a little more milk and butter added. Let them stay in the steamer for a few minutes to absorb the milk, if you mash them, then serve them. Scrub the skins well before working with them as they are often dirty.

BOILED POTATOES

An objection to steaming is that it takes longer than boiling. Often you will not have time to wait. You can get almost the same flaky effect from boiling potatoes, if you boil them properly. Select the smallest ones possible and, of course, choose ones as nearly uniform in size as possible. Wash them with a vegetable brush and drop them into boiling, salted water. Cook from twenty minutes to half an hour or until you can see, by testing them with a fork, that they are soft. Have no lid on the saucepan. When they are done, drain them, then put them back in the pan. Put them on the fire with the burner turned very low and the pan covered. Leave them there for several minutes to dry out the excess moisture. Serve them on a deep plate and cover with a napkin to keep their heat in.

Unless they are to be eaten plain boiled or mashed, it is better to boil potatoes several hours before they are to be used and to let them cool. They harden a little as they cool and become easier to dice or slice (for frying, creaming, making into an au gratin dish or for salad).

BAKED POTATOES

Baked potatoes need careful cooking. Scrub the potatoes first, with a vegetable brush, then rub the whole skin over with lard or vegetable fat. This is to lubercate the skin and to keep the potato from getting too dry. Have a moderate fire in the oven (too hot a fire will harden the skins and cook the potato unevenly). Medium sized potatoes will bake in three quarters of an hour. As soon as they are done, slash each one with a slit about two inches long (to let out the steam). Serve them in a covered tureen, with a piece of butter pushed into each opening.

STUFFED POTATOES

Stuffed potatoes are made from baked ones. Cut each baked potato in half lengthwise, scoop out the contents, and mix this

102.

together in a bowl with warm milk, butter, pepper and salt. Use just enough milk to moisten the potato. Put the potato back in the shells, set these in a shallow baking pan in the oven and leave them there until they are brown on the top. The oven should be about 450 degrees.

MASHED POTATOES

If you are in a great hurry to get potatoes boiled, pare them before you put them to boil and cut them in small pieces. Prepared this way, they will get soft in ten or fifteen minutes. To mash them, first drain them and set them back in their pan on the stove for a minute to dry. Then mash them thoroughly, getting out all the lumps. In a small saucepan, heat almost to the boiling point half a cup of milk and a tablespoon of butter seasoned with salt and pepper. Add this to the mashed potatoes, beat with a spoon until the mixture is light and serve in a covered dish.

If you want to serve mashed potatoes in a very attractive way, spread them after they are mashed over a pie pan. Set this under the grill of a hot oven until the top of the potato is uniformly brown. Garnish a steak platter, or a dish of chops, with this browned potato.

FRENCH FRIES FROM SCRATCH

Cut potatoes in strips or slice as thin as possible. Place in cold water until ready to fry. Heat cooking oil in a large, deep pot or deep fat fryer. Drain potatoes and dry well (wet potatoes will splatter in hot oil). Add them to hot oil and fry, stirring occasionally, until golden brown. Do not crowd while cooking. Drain on paper towels or crumpled newspaper. Serve in a basket to prevent sogginess. Salt to taste.

HASHED BROWN POTATOES

Hashed brown potatoes are an elaborated form of plain fried ones. They must be finely cut first (run them through a meat grinder if you have one). Mix them with a small ground onion, salt, pepper, and ground parsley. Melt butter or cooking fat in a frying pan (not more than a tablespoon for four potatoes) and when the fat is hot, drop the potatoes in. With a spatula, flatten the mass down into a roll at one side of the pan. When it is brown underneath, turn it while keeping the roll as compact as possible. Brown the second side and serve immediately.

POTATOES AU GRATIN

Potatoes au gratin are baked creamed potatoes, with cheese and bread crumbs added. Peel and cut into dice two or three boiled potatoes. Make a cream sauce with one tablespoon each of butter and flour. Add a cup of milk. When this is thick and seasoned, drop the potatoes into it. Grease a baking dish, put a layer of bread crumbs in the bottom of it, then a layer of creamed potatoes. On top of this put a layer of mild cheese cut into slivers. Repeat the layers until the potato is all used. Put a few bread crumbs on top. Set the baking dish, uncovered, in a hot oven until the top crumbs are brown.

When you are frying steak or chops, you can very easily cook potatoes with the meat but it will be necessary to have them sliced very fine so that the pieces will not be more than an eighth of an inch thick. A good plan is to cut each potato in strips lengthwise, then cut each strip into a number of small strips. Put these in the pan with the cooking fat about five minutes before you put the meat in. Salt them and let them cook with a moderately slow fire (with a lid on the pan). They will cook in their own liquid.

When you put in the meat, pile the potatoes to one side of the pan (as much away from the hottest flame as possible). Otherwise, you can take them out of the pan and heat them up again after the meat is cooked. Serve the potato strips as a garnish for the meat. Sweet potatoes are more decorative for this purpose than Irish ones.

RICE

Rice, to be dry and flaky, must be cooked rapidly in plenty of boiling salted water. Half a cup of rice will make about two cupfuls cooked. Wash the rice by holding it under cold running water in a wire colander. When the salted water is boiling fast, drop the rice in and leave the lid off the pan while the rice cooks. Twenty-five minutes boiling should be enough to make it soft. Drain it in a wire colander and turn it into a tureen. Put dabs of butter on top of it, then cover the tureen.

A half cup of rice will, when boiled, be enough for two persons. A simpler method of cooking can sometimes, depending on the rice, be found on the package directions.

MACARONI AND NOODLES

Cook macaroni and noodles just as you would cook rice unless you are cooking them in soup. Wash them first, break them up, then boil them rapidly for about 25 minutes. Drain them. Reheat them in a brown sauce or in tomato sauce with a piece of cheese melted in it. You can also simply fry them brown in hot butter and serve them with Parmesan cheese grated over them.

HOW MANY POTATOES TO USE

● Steamed or boiled, two small ones to a person.

● Baked, one large one or two small ones to a person.

● Stuffed, two to a person.

● Mashed, one large one or two small ones for each person to be served, with two more added.

● Fried, one or less for each person.

● Au gratin, one or less for each person.

● Raw fried, one small one for each person.

106.

HINTS ON POTATOES

BOILING POTATOES: Potatoes boiled in their skins can be made to taste liked baked potatoes if you put a large amount of salt in the cooking water.

GRILLED POTATOES: Try grilling potatoes for a change. Slice cooked potatoes lengthwise, brush with melted butter, sprinkle with salt and pepper. Broil under the broiler in the oven until brown.

MASHED POTATOES: Try mashing potatoes with the skins. They are very tasty and contain many more vitamins.

MILK IN POTATOES: When mashing potatoes, add hot milk as cold milk will make the potatoes soggy.

ROASTING POTATOES QUICKLY: Potatoes may be roasted more quickly if they are first washed in hot water and allowed to stand for a minute in it.

POTATOES DISCOLORED: To prevent old potatoes from becoming discolored when boiled, add a slice of lemon to the water. It is also preferable not to use an aluminum boiling pot for these vegetables as they will discolor more readily.

BAKING POTATOES: If the skins of potatoes are well washed and buttered before putting the potatoes in the oven, they will be a beautiful brown and crisp when baked. Also be sure to prick the skin before baking. This will prevent them from exploding in the oven.

VEGETABLES

Of vegetables in general, the most important fact to be remembered is that they should not be served with cream sauce. Peas, carrots, lima beans, string beans, asparagus, and even mushrooms are all too often merged into one individuality by being heated in a thick white sauce which calls attention only to itself. These vegetables have delicate flavors of their own and each one is distinct. It is only by developing the flavors that you can use them to advantage.

When the vegetables are new and green, their delicacy is, of course, more marked. Cook them the day they are picked, if possible, or at least before they are more than two days old. Peas, lima beans, string beans, carrots and asparagus should be put to cook in a covered saucepan with barely enough boiling salted water to cover them. Let them simmer until soft (the time will vary with the vegetable). Just before they are done, add a little butter. When this has been thoroughly absorbed, they will be ready to serve. Carrots, before being cooked, must be pared and cut into dice.

Any of these vegetables may be reheated, after being cooked until soft, in a frying pan with steak or chops. This will bring out their flavor and give them the tang of the meat. Mushrooms are so soft in their natural state that they will need only this one cooking to make them ready for the table. Cut them fine and leave them in the frying pan with the meat for five or six minutes.

There are more complex ways of reheating vegetables (either fresh or canned). One way is to make a sort of soup of an onion sliced and fried slowly in butter until it is soft. A cup of water is

108.

added and allowed to come to a boil. Put the vegetable in this (asparagus is especially good treated so) and as soon as the mixture is hot, turn it into a tureen to serve. Cover with bits of butter before taking to the table.

STEAMED VEGETABLES

This is a method of quick cooking any vegetable that helps preserve its flavor and vitamin content.

Chop or slice vegetables uniformly. Melt about a tablespoon of butter in the bottom of a sauce pot. Add salt and a bit of sugar. Stir in vegetables and coat well with butter mixture. Add a tablespoon of water and cover with a lettuce or cabbage leaf. Cover with a tight lid and cook on low heat until done.

For more pure flavor, you can cut vegetables and cook in a steamer placed over boiling water in a pot. The water should not touch the vegetables. They will cook in the steam. Add butter and serve.

BEETS

Beets, if they are new ones, will need from an hour to an hour and a half to soften. Old beets must cook for several hours. Before putting the beets to boil, wash them and cut off the tops (leaving about an inch of the stem on the beet). After they have softened in plenty of boiling salted water, drain them, plunge them for a few minutes into cold water and skin them. They are then ready to be reheated for the table.

This sauce is often used for them: Melt a tablespoon of butter in a saucepan, add to it a tablespoon of flour, blend the two, stir into them half a cup of vinegar and a tablespoon of sugar. Into this, when it has boiled, drop the sliced beets. Serve hot.

Beets may be warmed up in butter alone with lemon juice squeezed over them while they are in the pan.

CORN

Corn on the cob will cook in boiling salted water in about twenty minutes.

CABBAGE

If you are going to cook cabbage, cut it into quarters first and take out the hard center. Have salted water boiling hard in a wide cooking kettle. Drop the pieces of cabbage in and leave the lid off the pan while the cabbage cooks fast for twenty minutes. Cooked in this way, the cabbage will have scarcely any odor.

Drain the cabbage when it is done, and prepare it for the table by chopping it with a knife and spoon until it is minced. Then make a cream sauce. Cabbage is the one exception to the cream sauce rule. This is because its flavor is vigorous enough not to be dominated. Season the sauce and put the minced cabbage in it. Put the cabbage and sauce in a greased flat baking dish and set it under the flame of the oven grill until it is brown on top.

CELERY

Celery makes a dainty cooked vegetable. Like mushrooms, it can be cooked enough by including it in a frying pan with meat. Treated in this way, it will still keep some of its crispness and get brown as it cooks. If it is boiled in salted water for twenty minutes, it will be soft. Drain it (being sure to keep the cooking water to use for a sauce at another meal) and reheat it in a brown or a cheese sauce. You can also simply fry it in butter and add a half teaspoon of tomato sauce to it just before you take it from the fire. Celery needs a pungent seasoning.

CANNED VEGETABLES

Canned vegetables need only to be drained and reheated in melted butter, in a frying pan with meat or in a casserole combination.

BAKED BEANS

Dried navy beans must be washed and soaked over night in cold water. One cupful will make a medium sized baking dish full of baked beans. After the beans have soaked, drain them and cook them in boiling salted water until they are soft (which should be about an hour and a half). Set the oven at 400 degrees. Put the beans, with enough of their cooking water to cover them, in a shallow baking dish (or in a bean pot if you have one). Add two tablespoons of molasses and two slices of either bacon or salt pork. Put the baking dish or the pot in the oven and bake until the beans get brown and absorb most of the water around them. Keep adding hot water if they get dry before they are brown. They will require from one hour to an hour and a half to bake.

DRIED LIMA BEANS

Dried lima beans will not need to soak overnight. After you have washed them under running water in a colander, put them to cook in just enough boiling salted water to cover them.

Let them simmer with a lid on the pan for two hours or until soft. To serve them, pour off (and save for cooking purposes) all their water but a cupful. Stir a teaspoon of cornstarch with a teaspoon of cold water in a cup until the cornstarch is dissolved. Add it slowly to the beans and stir them until they come to a boil. Serve in a covered tureen.

TOMATOES

Fresh tomatoes make a very substantial dish when baked. Wash them, cut off a slice from the stem end, and scoop out a spoonful of the inside. Salt the hollow and fill it with crumbled bread which has been seasoned with salt and sweetened with a pinch of granulated sugar. Put the tomatoes in a shallow baking dish containing a cupful of hot water and bake in a hot oven (uncovered) until the tomatoes are soft and the bread crumbs brown. Canned corn or green beans of any kind may be used for a stuffing instead of bread.

Or you can fry tomatoes. Wash them and cut them into thick slices, making only three slices out of one tomato. Put these in a frying pan with two tablespoons of melted fat. Flour each slice and fry them until they are soft using a slow fire on top of the stove. Serve them either alone or on hot toast. If you like, you can make a sauce to go over them by mixing half a tablespoon of flour with the grease in the pan and then pouring on enough cold water to make a thin sauce. Add some chopped parsley and seasoning. Let the sauce come to a boil. Pour it over the fried tomatoes.

ONIONS

Onions may be stuffed and baked just like tomatoes. Tomatoes themselves make a good stuffing for the onions. Use only a teaspoon of stewed tomato to each onion. Bake the onions in a shallow pan in a little hot water or milk.

HOW MANY VEGETABLES TO BUY

● A standard can of vegetables will serve three or four persons.

● One cup of dried lima beans will make enough for two.

● One pound of green peas will serve two.

● One half pound of string beans will serve two.

● One pint of green lima beans (shelled) will serve three.

● Two medium sized carrots will serve two.

● One pound of beets will serve about three.

● Allow two or three ears of corn to a person.

● One large head of cabbage will serve four persons.

● One pound of tomatoes (or two or three large ones), when baked, will serve two. Two medium sized ones, fried, will serve two. Sliced, one large one will be enough for two.

● Allow one or two onions, either baked or stewed, to a person.

113.

HINTS ABOUT VEGETABLES

FRESH CELERY: Celery can be distinguished by its crisp white stalks and fresh bleached leaves. Choose celery with tender stalks that are not too stringy.

FRESH HEAD LETTUCE: Head lettuce, when fresh, is firm and heavy with no signs of brown on the outer leaves. Iceberg head lettuce is the most common lettuce in markets today, but this lettuce has fewer vitamins and minerals than other varieties of head lettuce.

FRESH SPINACH: Fresh spinach has tender, crisp leaves with stems that snap. It is high in iron and other minerals. It also has a lot of vitamins and is excellent as a lettuce substitute for tossed green salads.

FRESH TURNIPS: Turnips are not as popular as many other vegetables but are an excellent source of nutrients. They can be served in a variety of interesting ways. Turnips, when fresh, are neither wilted or pithy. They are heavy for their size and of good color. These vegetables, sliced thin, may be served with celery, carrots, and other raw vegetables along with a dip.

WASH VEGETABLES: Wash all vegetables thoroughly as soon as they come from the market. While dripping, place them in a plastic bag and store in the vegetable crisper of your ice box. When ready for service, they will be crisp and fresh.

114.

PEELING VEGETABLES: Deeply colored vegetables lose their coloring by over cooking. Never peel beets before cooking. Wash well and cut off all but one half inch of the stalk. Do not cut the root. If the root is cut off, the beet will "bleed" and lose color during cooking.

SALADS

The theory of salads is simple. It consists of serving in a cold, highly seasoned form any kind of food material that you have on hand.

Think of salad as something crisp and cold. The most succulent part of dinner. Plan it to fill its place adequately but not too well. A heavy fruit salad with mayonnaise would make your dinner top heavy unless the salad were to be salad and dessert in one. A fish or a meat salad would be inappropriate. Potato salad with dinner would not only be too heavy, but it would more than likely repeat the potato element which had been served with the main course.

Make your salads so that they will be easy to eat. Shredding the lettuce will help, and dicing the vegetables or fruit. Tomatoes, if they are served whole, should have their skins taken off first to make them soft enough to be cut with a fork.

There are two basic salad dressings. These tend to separate salads themselves into two main divisions. French dressing, made of an oil and an acid with seasoning is generally used with light salads (those made of lettuce alone or of lettuce with some light added element such as asparagus tips or string beans in small quantity). Mayonnaise goes with substantial fruit and vegetable salads, tuna fish, and salmon.

LETTUCE

As soon as you get lettuce home from the store, prepare it for salad making. Wash it under cold running water and separate the leaves. If it is head lettuce, cut off and throw away the stem. If it is Chinese lettuce (also called Napa cabbage), take off the outer leaves, but let the center of the stalk remain intact. This may be sliced down crosswise as you need it (as cabbage is sliced). Place the washed lettuce in a lettuce bag or wrap it loosely in a napkin and put it on ice. If there is no ice, keep it in a bowl of cold water and covered.

CELERY

Treat celery in the same way. Separate and wash every stalk. Cut off the leaves to be used for sauce making or in cream of celery soup. Save the centers of heart celery for serving as a relish on the table. Put away the smaller stalks to make into stuffed celery as an hors d'oeuvre at lunch. Slit the big stalks down lengthwise into two or three strips. This will make them crisp and curly. Keep the celery on ice.

CUCUMBERS

Cucumbers, when they are in season, may sometimes take the place of lettuce in salads. Wash the cucumber and run a fork lengthwise over the whole surface of the skin. Then peel the cucumber and slice it. You will find that the edges of each slice are attractively scalloped. Keep the slices in cold salted water for an hour before using them.

RADISHES

Radishes may be sliced or peeled and served whole.

TOMATOES

To skin tomatoes for a salad, wash them and hold over a burner with a fork or drop them into boiling water off the stove. Leave them for a few minutes, then take them out and plunge them into cold water. The skins will now come off easily. Set the tomatoes in the refrigerator to get cold and firm.

117.

CABBAGE

Cabbage, if it is to be used in salads, should be kept either in the refrigerator wrapped in a cloth (to keep its odor from the other food), or in some other cool place. To make it into cole slaw, slice it down crosswise at the head and chop it in a bowl. Mix it with boiled mayonnaise, sweetened with a little powdered sugar.

FRENCH DRESSING

French dressing is so easy to make that it is much better to mix it fresh each time you need it than to make it in quantity and set it away. It should not simply be poured over the salad ingredients. That would not mix it with them. It would leave the oil and the acid separate and the seasoning would be half with the oil and half with the acid. French dressing should be made and added to the salad all in one operation.

If the salad is to be of lettuce and a small quantity of some cooked vegetable (beets for instance), shred the lettuce after you have dried it in a napkin and put it in the mixing bowl. Pour a teaspoon of vinegar or lemon juice into the bowl and stir vigorously with a wooden spoon until the lettuce has been well moistened with it. Put a pinch of salt in the spoon, fill the spoon with oil, and with the fork, stir the oil until the salt is dissolved. Then add the oil to the lettuce and stir the salad again. Sprinkle with white pepper and paprika. Add the sliced or diced beets, toss them around once or twice to let them absorb the dressing (but not forcefully enough to force out their juices) and serve the salad at once.

Never mix lettuce with French dressing until just before you want to serve it. The acid will draw the water from the lettuce and wilt it. If you are going to serve a heavy salad of vegetables with

118.

French dressing (a salad in which the lettuce is only for garnishing), mix the vegetables with the dressing at least half an hour before the meal. This gives them time to absorb the oil and vinegar thoroughly. At the last minute, put the salad on lettuce.

VARIATIONS OF FRENCH DRESSING

Plain French dressing may be varied by the addition of new seasonings. Worcestershire sauce may be used with the vinegar mixing half and half. If you chop up a branch of parsley and a sour pickle or a stuffed olive, add them to the salad when you add the vinegar and you will have a vinaigrette dressing which will do very well to serve with left over fish or with a tart salad of apples and cream cheese.

With salads of fruit, lemon juice is better to use than vinegar because it is milder. With lettuce alone, vinegar will be better. Catsup, tomato sauce, ground onion, dry mustard, chopped capers and orange juice may all be used, with discretion, at different times. If the salad ingredients are insipid, try to supply piquancy with the dressing.

MAYONNAISE

Mayonnaise dressing may be mixed cold or boiled. There will be a difference in taste. Boiled mayonnaise, although it may have oil added to it after it cools, will lack the smoothness and the gliding quality of oil mayonnaise. It is much lighter in composition, softer and more delicate. For sandwich making, for fruit salads that are to be served with whipped cream after the dressing is added, and for salmon salad, boiled mayonnaise might be more palatable.

119.

BOILED MAYONNAISE

Boiled mayonnaise is made in this way: Cream together in a saucepan one tablespoon each of butter, sugar and flour. Then one half teaspoon of salt and one half teaspoon of mustard. Add the yolk of one egg, unbeaten. When the egg is mixed with the rest, add three fourths of a cup of milk slowly, stirring as you pour. Then set the pan over a slow fire and bring the mayonnaise gradually to a boil, stirring it continually. As it heats, add little by little a fourth of a cup of vinegar. The mayonnaise is done when it has boiled up once and is smooth. Set in a cool place. After it is cold you can stir oil into it, if you like, to make it richer.

OIL MAYONNAISE

To make oil mayonnaise that will not separate during the making, you have only to add the acid ingredient before you add the oil. This partly curdles the egg and makes it receptive to the oil. Put in a cold mixing bowl: a half teaspoon each of salt, dry mustard and powdered sugar. Add a pinch of white pepper and a pinch of paprika. Mix these seasonings and add to them one and a half tablespoons of either vinegar or lemon juice. Add to them the yolk of one egg and beat the whole with an egg beater. When it is blended, add the oil (preferably olive oil, but, lacking it, any reliable vegetable oil) at first by the tablespoon and then, as the mayonnaise thickens, in larger quantities. Altogether a cup and a half of oil may be absorbed by the egg. If the mixture will not thicken at first, which happens occasionally, set the bowl in the refrigerator for an hour or so. You will find the mayonnaise thick when you take it out again.

120.

VARIATIONS OF MAYONNAISE

With either boiled or oil mayonnaise as a foundation, you can make other dressings. Thousand island dressing is mayonnaise with a teaspoon of tomato sauce in it, either pickles or olives chopped, a branch of celery, and a teaspoon of capers. Tartar sauce is made by adding to mayonnaise a pinch of mustard, some chopped parsley, a teaspoon of onion juice, and a chopped hard boiled egg. For fruit salad, you can make a fluffy dressing by beating sweetened whipped cream into the mayonnaise.

Keep your mayonnaise in a covered glass jar or earthenware bowl in the refrigerator.

SALADS IN GENERAL

So a wide variety of kinds of salad is possible. You cannot divide salads into fruit, vegetable, fish, meat or plain lettuce because these all overlap. Vegetables might belong in your salad of cold chopped veal. A few pieces of tart apple would give flavor to your vegetable salad, fish salad might need vegetables in it, and plain lettuce is much improved by both meat and fish.

The question you have to decide continually is the question of assortment and flavoring: which dressing should the salad have? French dressing or mayonnaise or both?

You must take the matter of salad seriously. It will make a big difference whether the string beans are put together with oil and vinegar or with mayonnaise. Beets will lose all character if they are mixed with mayonnaise. Sometimes a salad will be quite without a crisp element when you might easily have added to it either celery or nuts.

Since flavor and seasoning are so important, you must be ingenious in distributing them. If, for example, you are making a salad of several kinds of fruit (for example, bananas, fresh peaches and Malaga grapes), instead of cutting the fruit all up and adding mayonnaise to it in a mass, make the salad interesting and unexpected by diffusing the dressing. In the bottom of the salad bowl, lay lettuce leaves. Put the bananas and slice them in thin strips lengthwise. Squeeze lemon juice over the strips and lay them on the lettuce. Then cut up the peaches into slices and stir them thoroughly with sweetened mayonnaise. Distribute them well over the bananas. Finally drop the grapes, sprinkled with lemon juice, on top of the salad. In this way, you see, the bananas will be covered with mayonnaise because they are covered with peaches. Yet they will keep their own lemon flavor too.

This scheme of double dressing may be applied to vegetable salads too. Let the vegetables stand for half an hour in French dressing. Then shred lettuce, mix it with mayonnaise, and stir it up among the vegetables. Serve with a dab of mayonnaise on top of the salad.

DESSERTS

Desserts, like soups and salads, must be adapted to dinner with a nice calculation of the need they are to supply. There are pies, custards, puddings and the like to give heaviness to a meal. Likewise, there are tarts, fruit whips, gelatine and the like to give delicacy.

Of all the cooked desserts, custards are the simplest and the most quickly made. They are made with milk, sugar, and a flavoring element. They are thickened with either eggs or corn starch (sometimes both).

PLAIN CUSTARD

To make a plain, eggless custard for two people, put half a pint of milk in a saucepan with a heaping tablespoon of sugar. Set this over a moderate fire. In a cup, mix half a tablespoon of corn starch with a tablespoon of milk. Stir the milk and the sugar until they just reach the boiling point. Then pour in the dissolved corn starch and turn the flame down low. Stir the custard for several minutes longer, then take it from the fire and add a quarter of a teaspoon of vanilla. Pour into custard cups or sherbert glasses to cool, and be ready to serve.

This will need some decorative feature, such as a teaspoon of canned cherries or apple jelly, or two or three slices of bananas in the center of each custard. Add these after it has cooled. Another possibility is to add coconut by scattering it over the top.

COFFEE CUSTARD

To make this same custard flavored with coffee, put half coffee and half milk in the saucepan with the sugar and proceed as before. Use fresh, strong coffee which has been well strained.

CHOCLATE CUSTARD

To make chocolate custard, put a tablespoon of cocoa in the saucepan first, add just enough milk to dissolve it and then gradually stir in the rest of the milk. Add the sugar and proceed as before. It will lighten and improve chocolate custard to beat half a dozen soft marshmallows into it while it is still hot. Garnish the cold custards with marshmallows cut into pieces.

EGG CUSTARD

Custards made with egg will, of course, have more nourishment in them. They are make in the proportion of two eggs to one pint of milk. If you omit one egg, you may substitute for it half a tablespoon of corn starch to supply the quota of thickening. Separate an egg, putting the white in a bowl ready for beating. Put the yolk in a saucepan. Stir the yolk and add to it a tablespoon of sugar. Then gradually add half a pint of milk. Put the saucepan over a medium fire and stir until the custard thickens. Never let it boil. Keep it at the simmering point. Add vanilla after you have taken it from the fire. Beat the white of egg, sweeten it with a pinch of sugar and pour the hot custard over it. Stir gently to let the white of the egg come to the top of the custard. Then pour the mixture into serving cups and set it away to cool. This is called floating island.

Coffee or chocolate custard may both be made with egg if you want them to have more body.

If you make a pint of custard and use only one egg, add the corn starch when the custard first reaches the bubbling point.

CUP CUSTARDS

For cup custards, use the same proportions as for boiled ones. Mix the custard in a bowl, putting in first the whole egg, then the sugar. Then add the corn starch, if one egg is omitted, or, if no egg is used, the flavoring. Lastly add the milk.

Dissolve the corn starch in the milk before adding it. When the materials are blended, pour them into small, buttered baking dishes. Set these in a pan of hot water and bake in a slow oven until a knife inserted in a custard will come out with a clean blade. Half a pint of milk will make two cups of custard.

PUDDINGS

A pudding is usually a heavier dessert than a custard. It is made with some dominant material (rice, bread or fruit). It may be steamed or baked.

Unlike custards, puddings are better baked in one mass and ready to be sliced into individual servings after they are cold. A pudding needs the richness that bulk cooking can give it.

Have your baking dishes of tin, aluminum or earthenware.

RICE PUDDING

Rice pudding is the most quickly mixed. Grease a baking dish and put in it one tablespoon of washed white rice to half a pint of milk. Add a pinch of nutmeg and three tablespoons of sugar.

Cover the dish and bake in a very slow oven until the rice is soft and has absorbed the milk. The pudding should have browned on top. This will serve two.

BREAD PUDDING

Bread pudding, made well, is far from being a common dish. Grease a small baking dish and put in it a cupful of crumbled bread (preferably not too fresh). In a bowl, beat the yolk of an egg with a cup of milk. Pour this over the bread and stir in a tablespoon of seeded raisins. Be careful to cover the raisins with milk and bread so they will not be exposed directly to the heat of the oven. Lastly, add half a cup of either brown or granulated sugar. Bake in a moderate oven until the pudding is set and brown. Then beat the white of an egg, slightly sweetened, and spread it over the top of the pudding. Return it to the oven and let the meringue brown. Serve the pudding either hot or cold. This amount is for two.

This is the basis of bread pudding. Using it, you may elaborate or change it as you will. You may put strawberry jam in it instead of raisins or cold cocoa instead of milk. Or you may bake it without fruit (using a fraction more sugar) and serve it with chocolate sauce. You can make the chocolate sauce by melting a cake of sweet chocolate in a quarter of a cup of milk. You could also make a marshmallow sauce for it out of ten marshmallows melted in a tablespoon of milk.

PEACH PUDDING

To make a pudding out of fresh or canned fruit, the simplest way is to use a plain muffin batter which is highly sweetened. If

126.

you want to make a peach pudding, for instance, pare and slice four peaches and squeeze over them the juice of half a lemon. Add a pinch of powdered clove. In a mixing bowl, beat one egg and add two tablespoons of sugar to it. Add next a half cup of milk. Sift in one cup of flour and a heaping teaspoon of baking powder. Beat, add the peaches, and pour into a greased baking dish. Bake in a moderate oven until the pudding is brown. Serve with a sauce made by cooking two tablespoons of sugar with four tablespoons of water and the juice of half a lemon. Thicken this sauce by adding, after the sauce has been boiling for a few minutes, a level teaspoon of corn starch dissolved in a little cold water. This quantity will serve four people.

DATE PUDDING

There are modifications of plain fruit puddings in which less flour and relatively more eggs are used. They are richer in composition. Such a pudding is made with dates and nuts. Beat one egg with a pinch of salt, add half a cup of sugar to it, half a cup of seeded dates, a quarter of a cup of chopped nut meats, and a tablespoon of flour sifted with half a teaspoon of baking powder. Beat them together and pour into a buttered baking dish. Bake in a slow oven for about twenty minutes or until the pudding is set. Serve with whipped cream. This quantity of ingredients will make only two portions.

The same pudding may be made with cooked prunes instead of dates or with apricots (or with any canned or fresh fruit). You can see that it is only a sweetened souffle with the addition of flour and baking powder.

APPLE PUDDING

There is another kind of fruit pudding that is made without flour, eggs or any liquid. It depends upon fruit juices for moistening. So watery fruits, like apples or pears, should be chosen for it. To make one of these with apples, butter a baking dish and put in the bottom of it slices of pared and chopped apples. Sprinkle them plentifully with granulated sugar and cinnamon. Cover them with raisins. Repeat the layers, leaving a layer of sugar on top. Cover the baking dish and bake in a quick oven until the apples are soft and glazed by the melted sugar. Take them out of the oven and set marshmallows over the top. Return to the oven to brown the marshmallows with the lid off the baking pan. Serve the pudding hot with a lemon sauce.

Four apples will make a pudding for four people.

FRUIT WHIP

Under the head of puddings might fall fruit whips, which are much too fragile in construction to be called puddings but which are baked and served with a sauce.

They are made with the white of egg alone. Beat the whites of two eggs very stiff. Add two tablespoons of sugar and two tablespoons of flour sifted with a teaspoon of baking powder. Drop in a cupful of chopped fruit (dates, prunes, peaches, cherries, bananas or berries) and pour immediately into a shallow greased baking dish. Bake in a slow oven until the egg rises and browns slightly. Serve cold in two sherbet glasses.

When a sauce is served with fruit whip, it must necessarily be as light as the whip itself. Whipped cream sweetened and colored pink with a few drops of gelatine flavoring is appropriate. So is a sauce made of candied cherries, chopped and cooked with half a dozen marshmallows soaked in milk.

Directions for making gelatine are always found on the package and they differ with different brands. Try to have several flavors of gelatine on hand so that you can make a little of each and get a contrasting effect. Orange and strawberry together will be eaten with twice the relish of either flavor alone.

Garnish your gelatine desserts with pieces of fruit, whipped cream, ground macaroons and marshmallows. Never use nuts as gelatine makes them soggy.

If you beat gelatine with an egg beater just as it is begining to harden, you can double the quantity of it. You can beat whipped cream into it or cold cocoa or coffee.

PIES

The most substantial of desserts is pie. It is not hard to make. It follows very definite and easy rules.

To make the crust, first have spread out in front of you on an adequately large table space a big bread board, a mixing bowl, a rolling pin, a pie pan, a small flour sifter, baking powder, lard (or any good vegetable fat), a glass of cold water, a fork , and a sharp knife.

First heat the oven to 350 degrees. Then grease the pie pan and sprinkle flour over the bread board.

Into the mixing bowl, sift two cups of flour, putting two teaspoons of baking powder and half a teaspoon of salt with the second sifterful. Add to this about half a cup of shortening and mix with fork or fingers until the flour has taken up the shortening and turned into a sort of coarse meal. Make a hole in the

129.

center of the flour and pour into it a very little cold water. Make the flour and water into a big ball, adding more water if necessary. When the ball is compact enough to be picked up, divide it in two and lay half of it out on the floured board. Flour the rolling pin and roll the dough out very flat (as nearly round as you can make it). Fit it over the buttered pie pan and with a sharp knife trim it around the edge of the pan. You are now ready to put the ingredients of the pie in place. Here are several pies you can fill it with:

FRUIT PIE

We will do this example with apples although it could be any fruit. Pare and cut into small pieces about four good sized apples distributing them evenly over the pie crust. In the bowl that you mixed the dough in, put half a cup of sugar and two tablespoons of flour. The flour is to thicken the juice made by the apples and melting sugar. With apricots, peaches or other less watery fruits, flour is not needed. Sprinkle the flour and sugar over the apples, add a pinch of either clove or cinnamon and a dab or two of butter. Then roll out the top pie crust and lay it over the apples. Trim the edge of the pan. Make indentations along the edge with a fork and cut two or three short slashes in the top of the pie to allow the steam to escape during cooking. Bake the pie for about half an hour in the oven at 350 degrees. Test it, when the crust is brown, by sticking a fork in one of the slashes. If the apples are soft to the touch, the pie is done. It will be better not to cut the pie until it has cooled.

CREAM PIE

A cream pie or lemon pie is made with only a lower crust. Prepare half the usual amount of dough and spread the crust over the bottom of the pan. Bake the crust in a 450 degree oven. When it is done and has partly cooled, add the cream or lemon filling (with its meringue) and reheat to brown the meringue.

The filling for a cream pie is the same as an egg custard. A pint of milk will make enough custard for one pie. If you like, you can add half a cup of shredded cocoanut to the custard before pouring it into the pie shell. Instead of pouring the custard over the beaten egg whites, put the egg whites on top of the custard after it is in the pie shell.

TARTS

Tarts may very easily be made out of left over scraps of pie dough. Roll the dough out very thin and press it down over the reverse side of a muffin pan which has been greased beforehand. Bake in a 450 degree oven. Take the shells carefully from the muffin rings and set them to cool. Just before serving them, fill them with fruit preserves or cooked custard. These same tart shells will do as patties for creamed oysters or meat.

CAKE

It is important to understand cake making in general before you begin trying individual recipes because as soon as you know the basic principles you can invent your own recipes easily.

There are two basic types of cakes: there is sponge cake which is made without shortening or liquid and there is butter cake which does use shortening and liquid.

131.

Both of these cakes must be beaten thoroughly. For both, the yolks and the whites of the eggs should be beaten separately. The yolks are added first and the whites are folded in last. For sponge cake and virtually all forms of butter cake, it is best to have the oven cold at the beginning of the baking. This gives the cake a chance to rise slowly before it starts to brown.

In order to mix up a cake quickly, you should have a small sifter (which measures approximately a cupful). You will also need a mixing bowl large enough to accommodate an egg beater without letting the batter splash over.

SPONGE CAKE

For sponge cake, this is the usual proportion: To one cup of flour, use one cup of sugar and three eggs. Add a pinch of salt and half a teaspoon of either lemon juice or vanilla flavoring. If you want to omit one egg, add a teaspoon of baking powder to the flour before sifting it. To make a white sponge cake, use the whites of eggs only, adding one extra egg white and add half a teaspoon of cream of tartar with the beaten eggs.

Mix a sponge cake in this way: Put the egg yolks in the mixing bowl with a third of a cup of cold water and beat them with an egg beater until frothy. Then beat in (gradually) the sugar, the flavoring, and the flour. As the mixture gets too solid for an egg beater, begin beating with a spoon. Lastly, gently fold in the beaten whites. Pour the mixture into a greased tube pan and place in a cold oven. Turn on at 350 degrees. The oven must be at a low temperature during the whole process of baking. The cake should bake in about three quarters of an hour. Stick a toothpick into the center of the cake to test it. If it comes out dry, the cake is done.Let it cool before removing from the pan.

BUTTER CAKE

A butter cake is mixed with a spoon. Mash the shortening first, until it is almost liquid, then add the sugar to it and mix the two thoroughly. Add the beaten egg yolks, beat vigorously for about three minutes. Then add the flour and the liquid alternately. Beat well with each addition. Add the flavoring, then stir in the beaten whites carefully and turn the batter out on greased layer cake pans or a loaf pan. Start in a cold oven. A layer cake should bake in less than half an hour. A loaf cake will need from three quarters to an hour. Bake at 350 degrees.

The proportions of a butter cake are these: To three cups of flour, use three teaspoons of baking powder, one cup of sugar, one cup of liquid (either milk or water—water will give the cake a lighter consistency), one third of a cup of shortening, a half teaspoon of salt and three eggs. Add a teaspoon of whatever flavor you like.

If you wish to make a white butter cake, leave out the the yolks of the eggs and replace with one additional egg white.

CHOCOLATE CAKE

To make a chocolate cake, use one half cup more sugar than for a butter cake and add two squares of unsweetened baking chocolate. Melt the chocolate over a slow fire, with enough water to cover it. You can use cocoa instead of chocolate. Use five tablespoons of cocoa and a half cup of shortening instead of a third of a cup. Cocoa lacks the fat of chocolate and the cake would otherwise be too dry. Stir either the chocolate or the cocoa in the batter just before you add the egg whites. Bake at 350 degrees.

SPICE CAKE

A spice cake is made by adding a teaspoon each of cinnamon and allspice, a half teaspoon of powdered clove, and, if you want, three tablespoons of chopped raisins. Combine these ingredients before you add the beaten egg whites. It is advisable to bake a spice cake in a loaf pan. For a quick icing, melt five tablespoons of butter and beat in half a cup of granulated sugar and two tablespoons of cinnamon. Spread this over the top of the cake when it is almost done. It will melt in the oven and form a glazed covering. Bake at 350 degrees.

CUP CAKES

For cup cakes, make half the usual amount of cake batter and pour it into greased muffin tins (making each ring about two thirds full). Cup cakes will bake in about twenty minutes. A good addition to cup cakes is a cup of chopped nuts put with the batter. Then when the cakes are done, decorate the top of each one with half a nut meat. Bake at 350 degrees.

COOKIES

Cookies are a form of butter cake made very stiff. They are mixed in virtually the same way as ordinary butter cake. They are to be rolled out in a thin sheet before they are baked (so a little bit of batter will go far). This is a safe estimate for a batch of two or three dozen cookies: one forth cup of shortening, three quarters of a cup of sugar, one egg, two tablespoons of milk and about two and a half cups of flour. The amount of flour must be indefinite because it depends on the growing stiffness of the batter. You can use either sweet or sour milk with cookies. If you use sour milk, dissolve in it a half teaspoon of baking soda before adding it to the batter. This is to neutralize the acid and render the milk sweet in taste.

To make cookies, mix the shortening and the sugar together, add the egg unbeaten (the aim in the making of cookie batter is for compactness rather than lightness). Then add the milk, half a teaspoon of vanilla or other flavoring and lastly the flour. Add the flour cup after cup until the batter is stiff enough to be taken up in your hands and formed into one mass. When it has reached this point, set it away for several hours or overnight. This will get it stiffer so that it can be rolled out very thin. When you are ready to bake it, work with the batter in small quantities at a time. Roll it out, cut it into shapes with assorted cookie cutters and bake them in a 450 degree oven. It will be necesery to grease the cookie sheet only once. You can bake many series of cookies one after another. Watch the cookies closely while they bake since they will brown in a few minutes. As each set is done, lay the cookies out flat on a big platter or a piece of paper and dust with powdered sugar while still hot. Cookie batter may be refrigerated for several days.

CHOCLATE COOKIES

There is a quick kind of chocolate cake that amounts almost to cookies in its finished form. It can be mixed and baked in about twenty minutes in all.

Here is the way it is made: In a small sauce pan, place one heaping tablespoon of shortening and a square of chocolate. Melt these over a slow fire. Meanwhile, beat an egg in a mixing bowl and add to it: one half cup sugar, a quarter cup of flour and a few drops of vanilla. Beat well, then add the melted shortening and chocolate. Pour the batter out on a greased pie pan. Cover the top of the batter with chopped nut meats and bake at 375 degrees until the top is set (about ten minutes). The batter will still be soft underneath when you take it out of the oven. Let it stand for a while, to cool, then cut it in squares like fudge. These cakes, as soon as they are cold, should be placed in a covered jar.

GINGERBREAD

Gingerbread follows rules of its own. It is a butter cake, but it is made with molasses instead of sugar and depends for its flavor upon spices.

Here is an easy recipe for soft gingerbread: Break an egg into a bowl and slowly stir into it three forths cup of molasses. Add a cup of flour with which are sifted one teaspoon each of cinnamon and ginger. Heat one half cup of water to the boiling point. Pour this over a tablespoon of butter and a teaspoon of baking soda in a cup. It will, in one operation, melt the butter and dissolve the soda. Add this liquid to the batter, beat well, and pour into a greased cake pan. Bake in a 300 degree oven for about half an hour. To test, an inserted toothpick will come out dry.

ICINGS

Cake icings may either be cooked or mixed cold. The cold ones are simpler, of course, and for most purposes they will be satisfactory.

136.

CHOCLATE ICING

For a cold chocolate icing to be used on a standard sized cake, take a cup of sugar and a half a cup of cocoa. Mix them and add, gradually, enough milk to make the icing of the right consistency to spread. There is danger of adding too much milk. Half a tablespoon is enough to start with. If you add too much, you will have to add more sugar and cocoa.

COLD WHITE ICING

To make a white icing, use a cup and a half of powdered sugar, a drop or two of vanilla or lemon juice and add milk to right consistency.

COOKED CHOCLATE ICING

A cooked chocolate icing is made like fudge. Put half a cup of grated chocolate in a sauce pan with a cup of sugar and one forth cup of milk. Let this boil without stirring for ten minutes. Remove from the fire and set in a cool place for five or ten minutes. Then add a small piece of butter and beat until thick enough to spread. A few marshmallows beaten with the warm icing will improve it.

COOKED CARAMEL ICING

Make a caramel icing with one cup brown sugar and one forth cup water. Let this boil until it will spin a thread when you drop it from the spoon. Beat, when it is partly cooled, and flavor with vanilla or lemon juice.

WHITE COOKED ICING

A boiled white icing will require the whites of two eggs. Have them beaten stiff and ready in a big bowl. In a sauce pan, cook together one cup of sugar and one third cup water. Boil them until they make a syrup that will spin a thread. Pour the syrup, as soon as it is done, into the beaten egg whites. Stir the mixture as you pour. Continue beating, after the syrup has been added until the icing gets thick. Add a few drops of vanilla before you spread it on the cake. Cocoanut or chopped nuts might be mixed with the icing or sprinkled over the cake after the icing is spread on. Candied cherries, sliced, make an attractive decoration.

LAST MINUTE DESSERTS

Besides these cooked desserts, there are dozens of quick desserts which can be gotten together in a matter of minutes. Cheese and crackers make a reliable one. Fresh fruit is always a wise dessert. So are nuts and cluster raisins. Or you may have stuffed dates, fruit cup, an elaborate sweet fruit salad, half a grapefruit with a teaspoon of jam in the center of it, salted nuts or after dinner mints. The limit is in your imagination.

ODD DESSERT HINTS

PIES

MOLASSES IN PIES: Pumpkin pies will bake a rich golden brown if a tablespoon of molasses is added to the filling for each pie. Molasses may also be substituted for sugar in cakes and cookies. It gives added flavor and supplies minerals that refined sugar has lost.

HONEY IN PIES AND STORING: Honey may also be substituted for sugar or molasses in pies, cakes and cookies. It will have a more delicate flavor than molasses, but yield the same consistency. When storing honey, try to keep it in a dark place as light helps cause honey to granulate.

TAPIOCA IN PIES: When making juicy pies, scatter a tablespoon of tapioca over the top before putting on the top crust. The tapioca keeps juice from running out and adds to the pie flavor.

MAKING MERINGUE: When making meringue for a lemon pie, stir two tablespoons of boiling water into it when it is ready to put on the pie and the meringue will not run.

CUTTING MERINGUE: If the meringue on a pie is not neatly cut, the portion does not look as appetizing when served. Try dipping the knife into cold water each time before cutting a portion.

PIE CRUST HINT: When too much water has been added in mixing pie crust, add a little flour and lard together. Add it to the mixture after blending. Flour added without the lard will make a tough crust.

FLUFFY PIE CRUSTS: A pinch of baking powder added to pie dough makes it light and fluffy. The baking powder should be mixed in with the flour before the shortening is added. You can also add a teaspoon of vinegar to the cold water used in mixing the dough to add flakiness to the crust.

BAKING PIE CRUSTS: Tin or aluminum pie pans are suggested for baking one crust pies because they bake quickly and brown the underside of the crust. For fruit pies which require longer, slower baking, an enameled or glass pan may be used.

SUGARING PIE CRUST: Sprinkle sugar over the lower crust of a two crust pie before adding the filling. The sugar will aid in preventing a soggy crust. Egg white, unbeaten, also may be brushed over the crust to aid in sealing it.

PIE TOP CRUSTS: A little sweet cream spread over the top crust of a pie before it is put into the oven will make the crust brown and flaky.

PIE'S RUN OVER: When a fruit pie runs over in the baking, try setting another pie pan half full of water under the pie rack. This saves the burnt odor and smoke of the burning juices. It also helps the cleaning job afterwards.

WHY PIE JUICES RUN: The juice in apple and berry pies run over because the oven is too hot. Turn down the temperature and let the pies cook slowly after the crust has begun to brown.

CUSTARD PIES: When baking custard pies, have the oven hot for the first three to ten minutes to bake the pastry quickly (so that the liquid will not soak through the crust).

CUSTARD PIE SHRINKING: When a custard pie shrinks from the crust, it has been baked in too hot an oven. The oven should be hot for the first five or ten minutes in order to bake the pastry so it will not become soaked with liquid. Then reduce the heat or the custard will boil.

MAPLE SYRUP IN PIES: For a change, when making a custard pie, cover the bottom crust with maple syrup before putting in the custard.

CAKES

GREASING CAKE PANS: It is always better to use shortening or lard for greasing bread and cake pans. Butter burns quickly where the other fats do not. The other fats are also cheaper.

CREAMING BUTTER: When creaming butter for cake, never take it directly out of the refrigerator. Allow it to stand before attempting to cream it. It will then cream more quickly and easily. Also, in creaming butter and sugar for a cake or cookies, a little hot milk added will aid the creaming process.

TESTING BUTTER: Good butter always burns quickly. Put a bit in a teaspoon and boil over a flame to test it. Butter that is not pure crackles and sputters. Do not use rancid butter in baking.

BEATING EGGS: When you beat eggs, do not half beat them and set them aside to be beaten again later. Always finish beating eggs before setting them aside and you will have better results. Also, it is best not to beat egg whites in aluminum bowls as they can darken and discolor the whites.

FROTHING EGGS: If a pinch of cream of tartar is added to whites of eggs when they are beaten, they will froth more quickly and stand up better.

SEPARATING EGGS: When you wish to separate yolks of eggs from whites, break them over a funnel and the whites will pass through leaving the yolks. Do not try this method of separating with older eggs, as the yolks weaken with age and have a tendency to break easily.

STORING EGG YOLK: When you have used a white of egg in a recipe and have no immediate use for the yolk, cover it with water. It can be kept for two or three days in the refrigerator.

CUTTING CAKE OR PIE: When cutting cake or pie, you can do a neater job if you dip your knife into cold water before inserting each time. This prevents sticking.

RESTORING CAKE: When cake becomes dry and hard, try the following: Soak it for a minute in cold milk and rebake it in a 250 degree oven. It will taste almost like new. You can treat stale bread in the same way.

142.

FRUIT IN CAKES: To prevent fruit falling to the bottom after you have stirred up your cake, add one teaspoon of vinegar at the end. You will not taste the vinegar in the cake and the fruit will not sink to the bottom.

ANGEL FOOK CAKE BEATER: Use a flat wire egg beater when beating the eggs for angel food cake. The eggs must be as light as possible and this kind of a beater gets more air into the egg whites than any other form of beater.

SPONGE CAKE SUGGESTION: Before placing a sponge cake in the oven to bake, try sprinkling a little white sugar over the top. This forms the rich brown looking crust that makes it so tempting.

TURNING CAKES: Always turn a cake upside down and ice the bottom, as the bottom is undoubtedly smoother and will ice better than the top.

FROSTING TIP: If frosting thickens before it cools, it will harden on the cake. If it hardens and is still warm, add two teaspoons of boiling water and beat until cold. If the frosting fails to thicken and is cold, add one forth cup sifted powdered sugar and heat until the sugar is thoroughly blended.

BOILED FROSTING: If syrup is not boiled long enough or too long, boiled frosting will be a failure. Do not pour the syrup over egg whites while it is boiling. Beat the frosting until quite stiff.

143.

PREVENT ICING FROM SUGARING: When making cooked cake icing, add a pinch of salt to the sugar and the icing will not grain and turn to sugar.

BETTER CAKE FROSTING: Frosting will more easily adhere to cake if a little flour is dusted over top of the cake before the frosting is put on.

SMOOTHING ICING: A knife dipped in hot water will smooth the edges of the iced cake.

SIMPLE CAKE BAKING: When making a cake, don't dirty all the dishes in the cupboard. Simplify in this way: Cream butter and sugar in a mixing bowl. Add egg yolks, saving whites in a smaller bowl to add later on for frosting. Then measure flour and baking powder in sifter and sift onto a clean paper. Sift back and forth into greased pan for three or four times. Put milk or liquid into same cup used for flour. In this way you save washing dishes.

CREAMING BUTTER: We all know that it takes time to cream butter when baking. It is far better to take the time than spoil the cake. Therefore, never melt the butter instead of creaming it. Melted butter makes a soggy cake.

BEATING CAKE: Don't beat your cake too much if you are using bread flour instead of pastry flour for mixing.

EGG SUBSTITUTE: When making cake, if eggs are scarce add one half teaspoon extra of baking powder per egg short.

144.

USE PASTRY FLOUR: Your cakes will be much lighter if you use pastry flour. If you must use bread flour in making a cake that calls for pastry flour, use a little less of the bread flour than the recipe calls for.

SMOOTHING CAKE BATTER: If the flour in the cake batter is lumpy, put the batter through a fine sieve and then pour it into the tins for baking.

PREPARING CAKE TINS: When preparing cake tins, use clarified dripping or lard in preference to butter which is likely to burn. Butter is also likely to make the cake sticky, owing to the salt and water butter contains.

SPONGE CAKE PAN: Never grease the pan in which you are going to make a sponge cake. Instead, line the pan with ungreased paper.

POURING BATTER: When filling cake pans, pour the batter into the corners and sides of the pans (leaving a slight depression in the center). When baked, the cake will be perfectly flat on top.

BAKING CAKE: When baking cake, arrange to have nothing else in the oven and place the cake as near the center of the oven as possible. This will give even cooking.

BROWNING CAKES: To brown a cake, place a basin of cold water in the oven just before the cake is put in. This will prevent burning and the cake will be a rich brown color.

TIME CAKE BAKING: When baking cake, time should be divided into quarters. The first quarter should rise, the second quarter should begin to brown, the third quarter it continues browning, and the last quarter it shrinks from the pan and continues browning.

CAKE BURNING: When baking a cake, if it seems to brown too quickly, reduce the heat and cover the cake. The baking will continue and the browning will stop.

REMOVING CAKE FROM PANS: If you find difficulty in removing cakes from the pans, try this method: When you remove the cake from the oven, stand the tin on a damp cloth for a moment. You will find that this will help the cake to slip out when you turn the pan over.

LOOSENING CAKE IN PAN: A cake which sticks to the tin may be loosened by placing the tin over a bowl of boiling water.

POTATOES IN CAKES: Next time you make a cake, add half a cupful of mashed potatoes to the other ingredients and see how rich and light a cake will result. If it is to be a white cake, add the potatoes to the creamed sugar and butter. If it is a yolk of egg cake, put in the potatoes after the yolks have blended.

MISCELLANEOUS

SOAKING RASINS: Always soak raisins before putting them in breads, cakes and pies. Otherwise they will absorb water and dry out the end product.

146.

RAISINS SINKING: If you are annoyed by having raisins or currants sink to the bottom of a cake, put them in a pan and set over a slow fire. Stir occasionally so they will not burn. When heated, add them to the batter.

RASINS STICKING: Raisins will not stick to a food chopper if the chopper is dipped into hot water before the raisins are put in.

BAKING BANANAS: Baked bananas over which lemon juice has been squeezed are especially tasty when served with baked meats (particularly with baked ham).

PRESERVING BANANAS: If lemon juice is squeezed over bananas after they have been sliced, they will not discolor.

CHOOSING BANANAS: Bananas are picked when green and ripened during shipment. In choosing this fruit, one is apt to select fruit not ripe enough because of their fresh appearance. Bananas are not really at their best until they begin to show a tinge of brown along the seams of the skin. You must be sure that the stem end is still solid and not beginning to soften.

CANDY TIP: Never scrape the sides of a pan when making candy and do not stir what has cooked onto the sides of the pan. A few sugar crystals stirred in from the sides may cause the whole mixture to granulate.

SUGAR FOR CANDY: When making candy, granulated sugar is preferred as brown sugar has molasses added and powdered sugar is more expensive.

MAKING FUDGE: Try beating fudge with an egg beater instead of a spoon. It will mix more quickly and will be creamier as a result. Also be sure to first pour the fudge from the pan into a cold bowl before beating. To prevent fudge from boiling over in the pan while cooking, try rubbing butter around the top of the pan and the fudge should not boil over.

SHIPPING FUDGE: To ship homemade fudge successfully, pour it while warm into a tin pan which has been lined with several thicknesses of wax paper. Leave sufficient paper to cover the top adequately and the fudge can be lifted out by means of it. The candy will then stay fresh for a week or more.

BAKING COOKIES: If the pan is turned upside down and cookies are placed on the bottom of the pan, they will bake an even brown.

DROP COOKIES: When making drop cookies of any kind, drop the spoonfuls of dough in well greased muffin tins. Instead of spreading, they will rise up and make nice uniform sized cookies.

SURPRISE COOKIES: Put two cookies together with marshmallow cream, ground figs or peanut butter and the cookies will be a special treat to everyone.

SOFTEN COOKIES: Almost any cookie will get hard after it is cool. To soften them, shut tightly in a covered tin or jar. It will take a few days for them to soften. If you want to soften them more quickly, set a cup of boiling water in the box with the cookies and the steam will soften them. You may have to renew the boiling water once or twice.

COOKIE JAR HINT: Put hot cookies in a crock with the skin of a orange or lemon. It will lend a very delicate flavor to the cookies.

ORANGE PEEL IN COOKIES: Grated orange peel is the best addition possible to molasses cookies or gingerbread. It gives a delicious, elusive flavor.

WOODEN SPOONS: For stirring and beating, you will find wooden spoons more satisfactory than metal ones.

METAL SPOONS: Use a metal instead of a wooden spoon when cutting and folding eggs into a cake.

SMOOTHING BROWN SUGAR: Brown sugar that is lumpy may be made smooth by allowing sugar to steam in double boiler until smooth.

LEMON JUICES: When the recipe calls for the juice of one lemon, it is safer to use three tablespoons of juice since this fruit varies greatly in the amount of juice to each lemon.

CUTTING MARSHMALLOWS: Always cut marshmallows with scissors and keep dipping the scissors in hot water frequently while cutting. This prevents the marshmallow from sticking.

WASHING SIEVES: Wash flour sieves with water to which a little bicarbonate of soda has been added. Never wash them in soap suds as the soap is likely to adhere to the fine meshes.

BUTTER SUBSTITUTE: If one half cup of butter is required in making a cake and you have only one fourth cup, add three tablespoons of sour cream and you will have a light, fluffy cake.

SOUR MILK IN CAKES: Sour milk may be used just the same as sweet milk in cake if one third of a teaspoon of soda is added to each cup of sour milk. After that, use baking powder just as though sweet milk has been used.

EVAPORATED MILK: Evaporated milk, diluted with an equal measure of water, may be used in any recipe in place of fresh milk.

BAKING POWDER SUBSTITUTE: Two teaspoons of cream of tartar and one scant teaspoon of baking soda are equal to three teaspoons of baking powder.

SOUR MILK SUBSTITUTE: When using sour milk in a recipe that calls for sweet milk, substitute half a teaspoon of baking soda for one teaspoon of baking powder.

BAKED APPLES: Apples that are to be baked should be pricked with a fork before being placed in the oven. If you do this, you will find they will not break while cooking.

CANNED CHERRIES: When using the canned red sour cherries for pie, use a few drops of extract of almond to bring out the fresh cherry taste.

DRIED CURRANTS: To clean dried currants, roll them first in flour. Then wash them in cold water and spread them out to dry. Roll again in flour before using.

SEEDING RASINS: Before seeding raisins, pour boiling water over them and let them stand a few minutes. Then drain them and the seeds will come out easily.

150.

ADDING RASINS: Never add raisins, currants, fruit or nuts to a cake until the beaten eggs have been added. Add them before adding milk. This way they will not sink to the bottom.

HIGH ALTITUDE COOKING: For cooking in high altitudes where the atmospheric pressure is much less than at or near sea level, certain changes must be made in a few of the ingredients. Eggs and flour must be increased, as they possess high resistive tenacity, while sugar and fats must be decreased because they have little tenacity and are liable to cause baked mixtures to fail or break apart.

Mix all doughs thoroughly and have them stiffer than in lower altitudes. A biscuit dough should be nearly as stiff as a bread dough. Use three tablespoons less per cup of sugar than the low altitude recipe calls for and two tablespoons less fat.

Boiled icing and candies need to cook one minute longer. Navy beans should be soaked over night in cold water so they will soften when boiled.

ALMOND FLAVOR: Almond extract added to vanilla produces another delightful flavor. Equal quantities of vanilla, almond and lemon also make a delicious flavor.

SOURING MILK: When making sour milk cakes and you have no sour milk on hand, add to a cup of sweet milk either a teaspoon of lemon juice or a teaspoon of vinegar and the milk will sour quickly.

SCALDING MILK: When scalding milk in a double boiler, it is usually at the right temperature when the water in the lower part of the boiler comes to a boil.

WHIPPING CREAM: When whipping cream in a warm place, put the bowl of cream in a pan of cracked ice. It will whip more easily. To make whipped cream go farther, put a ripe banana through a potato ricer, add the juice of half a lemon, a teaspoon of powdered sugar, and a pinch of salt. Fold into the white of an egg beaten stiff. Set in the refrigerator to chill and, when it is to be used, add to it what cream you have. Be sure to whip the whole thing again after adding new whipping cream to the mixture.

SOME ROUGH DRY WEIGHTS: Two cups granulated sugar weigh about one pound. Four cups pastry flour weighs about one pound.

MEASURING HONEY: If the measuring cup is greased for the measuring of molasses or honey, every drop of it will run out easily.

HOUSEKEEPING

HOUSEKEEPING

No one can tell you how to keep your house and no one should. A person's house is the place they live and it should reflect the style and comfort that they like.

One person may like to dust their home once every week. Another person may dust much more often and another less. You should do what you feel best with.

In light of this, the best this book can do is give you helpful household hints on individual cleaning and caretaking operations. Hopefully, these hints will prolong the life of many of your household articles and go a long way to making your housekeeping easier and more economical.

SEWING HINTS

SAVE BUTTONS: When an article wears out, try removing the buttons. Thread them together and store away for future use. All matching buttons will then be easily located.

BIAS TAPE: After breaking the paper open on bias tape, it tends to unwind and fall on the floor. Slip a rubber band on and you can hold the tape in place after cutting off the desired length. It will then always be straight and ready to use.

FABRIC SCRAPS: When making an article, never destroy the scraps. Later they may be used to make patches or pockets or even a quilt.

SEWING BUTTONS: Buttons which are to go through button holes should never be sewed flat to the garment. A shank should be made by laying a pin over the top of the button and sewing over it. Pull the pin out when sewing is finished and your button will not be too tightly fastened to the garment.

BUTTON THREAD: Heavy crochet cotton is excellent to use when sewing on the buttons on work clothes. It will stand much more resistance before giving way than ordinary thread.

BUTTONS ON FINE FABRICS: If you are sewing large buttons on fine material, use a small flat button on the inside of the material to prevent tearing a hole. This will secure the buttons better than using a heavy backing fabric to secure them.

155.

FASTENING BUTTONS: The buttons on a woolen or knitted coat sometimes tear away from the fabric, leaving a hole. To prevent this, place a button of equal size at the back as for fine fabrics. Sew right through, thus fastening both buttons with the same stitch.

SEWING BASKET: There are a few handy items to keep in a sewing basket which will make mending much easier. A small magnet is very useful in picking up small pins and needles. Rubber bands are also handy to keep the basket in order. Secure ribbons, tape, etc with rubber bands to prevent unravelling. They can also be used to secure spools of thread and darning cotton. There will be no more tangles to pick through.

CROCHET NEEDLE: Keep a cork on the end of the crochet needle when not in use and the needle will not snare other contents or work through the basket.

NEEDLES: If threading the needle is a strain on your eyes, try using an embroidery needle instead of a regular sewing needle. The long eye is much easier to thread and takes away a lot of eye strain.

DULL NEEDLES: To sharpen a dull sewing needle, run it through ordinary steel wool a few times and it will sharpen the point. Some pin cushions also have a sharpening aid (usually a bag filled with sand). To sharpen needles with this, run the needle (or pin) through five or six times and the burrs should be removed.

SORE FINGERS: In sewing tightly woven fabrics and in quilting, a rubber finger cot worn on the index finger will enable you to pull the needle through the fabric easily. It will save sore fingers and make the job much easier.

MENDING LACE: To mend fine lace curtains, starch a piece of mesh as similar to the curtain as possible. Cut the starched patch one inch larger than the place to be mended. With a warm iron, press it over the hole. If done carefully, it will be difficult to detect the patches. Another novel method of mending a hole in lace is to put a piece of paper under the hole and stitch on the machine until the hole is filled. Then pick out the paper. Use very fine thread for the stitching.

MACHINE DARNING: Table linen and house linen can be easily darned with a sewing machine. The presser foot should be removed and with needle and shuttle threaded, the fabric can be moved backwards and forwards while the machine works row by row of stitching closely set. When the hole and surrounding thin fabric are covered in one direction, the article should be turned half way around so that a similar set of rows of stitching may cross the first at right angles.

HOW TO BASTE: Baste with dark thread on light materials and white thread on dark. The lines will be much easier to follow.

GATHERING FABRICS: When gathering, use two single threads from ¼ to ½ inch apart. Then in stitching the gathered section to the straight one, stitch between the two rows of gathering threads. This prevents the material from pushing along and forming pleats under the pressure foot.

HEMSTITCHING: You can draw threads for hemstitching quite easily if you wet a small brush and rub it over a cake of soap until you get a lather. Then scrub over the threads you wish to draw.

FRENCH SEAMS: Before making French seams, remove selvedges. They are likely to shrink in washing and pucker the finished garment.

SCRAP SHEETS: When sheets become thin, cut them up and use for household rags, pillow cases and curtain linings.

VELVET: When you want to cut velvet for a garment, lay your pattern on the wrong side of the fabric and be certain you lay all pieces to be sewn together in the same direction (otherwise the nap will appear darker on some of the pieces).

LINT: It is usually difficult to brush lint from woolen garments. Try a dry sponge and see how easily you can get it off.

158.

TINTING AND DYEING HINTS

RESTORING COLORS: To make a faded garment white, it should be washed in boiling cream of tartar water (allow one teaspoon of the powder to a quart of water).

DYEING FABRICS: Wash carefully all fabrics to be dyed and see first that all spots and stains have been removed. Before dyeing or tinting curtains or garments, run a few threads of white cotton through the ends so that they are dyed with the rest of the material. After dyeing, they may be pulled out and rolled on a spoon to be used for mending or hemming. They will exactly match.

SETTING COLORS: Salt is especially effective in setting browns, blacks, reds and pinks. Use in the proportion of 2 cups of salt to 1 gallon of hot water. Immerse the garment into the hot water letting it remain until cold. For blues, use vinegar in the proportion of half a cup of vinegar to a gallon of water.

SETTING GINGHAM: To set colors in ginghams, put ½ cup of vinegar, ½ cup of salt and one small teaspoon of alum in a pail of lukewarm water. Soak the garment in this for one hour before washing. Be careful to leave it out in the sun only long enough to dry it.

DISSOLVING DYE: When dissolving dye, either in cake or powder form, place it in a small cloth bag. In this way it saves the usual task of straining and no chance of small undissolved

159.

parts. It will also float and when the desired shade has been obtained, it can be easily removed.

BLUE WATER: When making blue water, add a little common salt. This helps distribute the color evenly and prevents streaking or patching.

TINTING CURTAINS: Curtains or laces may be easily tinted beige by rinsing in tea water. Use 1 tablespoon of tea for each pint of boiling water. Test with a small piece of goods until the desired shade is obtained. Watch the length of time. The goods obviously must be left in longer when a light shade is wanted. The color will not be as deep after drying as it is when it is wet.

DYEING NAVY BLUE: Add one fourth package of black to a package of navy blue dye if you wish a garment to dye a good deep navy blue.

YELLOWED: One method for whitening yellowed clothes is to place a slice or two of lemon in the boiler in which the clothes are boiling.

160.

IRONING HINTS

With the easy care fabrics of today, ironing is not as essential as it was twenty years ago. However, natural fabrics are still very prevalent and increasing in popularity. We have therefore included a few suggestions to make the ironing job easier.

IRONS: To keep your iron in good shape, it is necessary to keep its ironing surface clean and smooth. One technique is to rub it with a piece of wax tied in a cloth. Afterwards scour with a piece of paper or cloth strewn with coarse salt. Another method is to sprinkle some salt on a newspaper and smooth and clean the iron before each use.

IRONING BOARDS: When covering an ironing board, use an old sheet (preferably white or at least colorfast). Try tacking the cover on the board while the fabric is wet. It will then dry gradually and be absolutely tight and smooth.

IRONING CLOTHES QUICKLY: If you wish to iron clothes soon after they are dry, sprinkle with hot water. They will dampen more quickly and evenly than if cold water is used.

IRONING TABLE LINENS: Use as few folds as possible in ironing. Most of the pieces may be rolled to avoid creases. Long tablecloths may be folded once and then rolled on a pole. Newspapers tightly rolled make good poles for small pieces. Cover with white paper until used. This also saves space in the linen drawer. When sprinkling linen napkins, try just dampening every third piece and stack between the dry napkins.

IRONING UNBLEACHED MUSLIN: When ironing new unbleached muslin, it irons easier and better if a bath towel is placed under the material.

WASHING HINTS

There are a few general rules to follow when washing fabrics either by hand or by machine. If using a machine, be certain to follow the directions (not overloading or over soaping). If washing by hand, check the manufacturers suggested washing directions on the garmet and you will receive much better service from the fabrics. For presoaking, it is not wise to soak clothes in hot water and leave them in it until the water is cold because cloth fiber expands in warm water and contracts in cold. In this way it will hold in the dirt. Make a suds of cold water if you want to soak fabrics for a length of time. Check clothing for holes and tears *before* you wash and mend immediately as the problems will usually worsen with the agitation of washing.

CHIFFON: To easily clean light chiffon or lace which is attached to a darker background fabric, simply lay the item over a heavy bath towel and scrub. The towel absorbs the water.

CORDUROY: When washing cotton corduroy , wash it thoroughly until the water is clear and hang it smoothly on a clothes line without wringing or squeezing. Let it drip dry. Then turn inside out and press on a towel with a hot iron. The corduroy will look like new.

COLORED COTTON: When washing colored cotton for the first time, put about one tablespoon of salt in each quart of water used. Use vinegar in the same proportion in the rinse water. This will set and brighten the colors. Also remember to use moderate water temperatures for washing colored materials. It is a good idea to turn the garments inside out when drying and the colors will stay bright much longer.

FEATHER ITEMS: Choose a bright, windy day to wash feather items. Fill the wash tub with hot suds and plunge the article into the suds. Put through several washings, shaking briskly, then hang on the line in the open air. When perfectly dry, shake well. After being washed in this way, the articles should be hung in the warm fresh air daily for a week. Never directly in the sun, though, as heat takes the oil out of the feathers and causes them to dry out and loose their loft.

LINENS: Remove all stains from table cloths and napkins before putting them into the wash. For white tablecloths and nap-kins, soak overnight in water to which a tablespoon of wash-ing soda has been added to each gallon of water. Wring out in the morning, then wash, and you will find the spots gone. Washing frequently sets the stains and if not soaked prior to washing they become very difficult to remove.

RIBBONS AND TIES: Don't put ribbons and ties into the ordi-nary wash. Make a bowl of sudsy water and lay the ribbon or tie flat on the table. Sponge it with the suds. Dry it flat on the table. Before it has started to dry, run your hand over it to be sure all air bubbles are out and less ironing will be required.

COLORED RIBBONS: Make a lather of cold or lukewarm water and fine soap. Wash by sousing up and down and squeezing.

164.

Do not rub, pull or twist them and they will not stretch out of shape. Very soiled pieces may be washed by running in good suds with the palms of the hand. Rinse several times in soapy water of the same temperature as the wash water. Then rinse one or two times in cold water. To quickly freshen silk ribbons, dip in a solution of white sugar and water. The ribbons will dry as if somewhat starched.

SATEEN: Add a little borax to the rinse water in which sateen or other cotton material with a glossy finish is placed. The shiny surface will be retained much longer.

SILKS: To clean pongee, tussah and novelty silks, wash them in lukewarm water and good soap. Instead of rubbing, scrub with a soft brush. Rinse in at least three waters.

PRINTED SILKS: First buy printed silks in which fast colors are guaranteed. Make a lukewarm suds of mild soap. Never use water over 110 degrees (either for washing or rinsing). Never apply the soap directly to the print. Wash by squeezing through the soap suds. When clean, rinse well and dry between two bath towels. When almost dry, press with a warm (not hot) iron. Protect the garment when ironing with cheesecloth or a piece of transparent paper. If you find the colors fading, make a rinse water up with a tablespoon of vinegar added. This will help set the colors.

WHITE SILK: When washing white silk, rinse in a solution of one teaspoon of grain alcohol to one quart of water. This will preserve the silk's luster.

SILK SLIPS: When washing a silk slip, the kind to be worn under silk or voile dresses, if the slip is starched a little the dress will not stick to it in an annoying manner.

SILK HANDKERCHIEFS: Silk handkerchiefs should be washed in lukewarm water and dried in the house. Use borax and little or no soap. Wash colored handkerchiefs in cold or tepid water and dry in the house or in the shade.

BLACK SILK: To clean, brush the silk thoroughly and wipe with a cloth. Then lay flat on a board or table and sponge well with cold coffee thoroughly strained (preferably through a handkerchief). Sponge on the side intended to show and allow to become partially dry. Then press on the wrong side. Experiment with thei method on a small piece of black silk and you will never use any other method.

SUEDE: To clean a suede jacket, shoes, etc., go over the entire surface with a piece of very fine sandpaper.

WOOLENS: To wash woolens, take one gallon cold water, two tablespoons of ammonia, and any mild soap. Rinse in blue water and hang out to be dried in the wind. Strong soaps and soap powders shrink and harden woolens. They also injure colored materials and cause yellowing. Hard rubbing also injures woolens so use a kneading motion in washing.

CLOTHING CARE

Do not overwear clothing is the advice of laundry experts. Frequent washing does much less harm than the vigorous treatment needed for very soiled clothes. To wash all articles more often, with less dirt to be removed each time is better for the life of the fabric than to wash more strenously at longer intervals.

Organizing your clothes hangers and using shoe trees increase the life of the articles. Care in putting away is worth more than pressing. Also, if the clothes you wear are looked over each time before they are put away, brushed, buttons tightened, etc., your wardrobe cannot help but be neat and in good condition at all times.

PREVENT YELLOWING: To prevent white clothes that are to be packed away from becoming yellow, dip a sheet in bluing water (use enough bluing to make the sheet quite blue), then spread the sheet after it dries and place over the clothing to be stored.

MOTHS: Moths will not come near clothes sprinkled with turpentine and will not breed in closets or drawers which have been sprinkled with turpentine.

POCKETS: To prevent the sagging of pockets of a new sweater, sew a piece of elastic inside the top pocket from one side to the other. The elastic will pull the pocket back in shape and it will never sag.

CLOTHING SHINE: When a dress suit of dark serge becomes shiny with wear, sponge it with hot vinegar and press it in the usual way. No odor of vinegar will remain, the shine will disappear, and the material will be much improved in appearance. The vinegar will leave no stain.

OLD CLOTHES: Clothes that you are not wearing will do someone some good if you will pass them along to those who need a little bit of help. There are many agencies that will collect donations directly from your home.

168.

SHOE CARE

ALTERNATE SHOES: To alternate two pairs of shoes is more economical than to wear one pair continuously. If the same pair is worn daily, they will wear out much faster because the moisture from skin never really dries out. By alternating every other day, you will extend the life of your shoes.

NEW SHOES: Sprinkle new shoes inside with talcum powder. They will be more comfortable during the breaking in process. New shoes should also be shined before wearing to prevent scuffing and to seal the leather.

DRYING SHOES: Drying wer shoes over a heater often spoils them. Heat causes the leather to crack and dry very hard. Dry your shoes indoors without extra heat applied. Also insert shoe trees or paper so they will keep their original shape.

MILDEW IN SHOES: To prevent shoes from mildewing in a dark closet during warm, damp weather, keep them on shoe trees or studded with paper and placed in a well ventilated and dry place. If any mildew is found, wash it off with warm water and soap or simply wipe off and dry the leather.

PATENT LEATHER: Patent leather shoes should be treated very carefully if they are to be kept in good condition. The

SUBSTITUTE SHOE POLISH: Lemon juice makes a good substitute for shoe polish. Sprinkle a few drops on either black or brown shoes. Rub briskly and this will give them an excellent polish in an emergency.

DARKENING BROWN SHOES: Brown shoes may be made darker by rubbing them with milk to which a few drops of ammonia have been added. This will dry very quickly. The shoes should then be polished with a clean dry cloth.

SCUFFED SHOES: When shoes become scuffed and peeled, rub them with the white of an egg. It will paste the broken pieces down flat and take away that scuffed look.

SUEDE SHOES: To clean suede , use a cheap bath sponge. This is said to be effective and does not mar the finish or texture of the pelt as does a brush.

170.

STAINS

CHOCOLATE: Chocolate stains, if not properly treated at first, are very difficult to remove. The best way is to make a solution of borax and hot water. Place the stained material over the opening of a bowl and pour the hot solution over the stains.

COFFEE: To remove coffee (and tea) stains, cover with glycerine and let stand three hours. Then wash with soap and cold water. Repeat if necessary.

FRUIT STAINS: If attacked when fresh and still damp, most fruit stains will come out when water is used. Never apply soap at first, as this can set the stain. Pour boiling water through white or colorfast materials. Certain fruit stains are quite stubborn (like berry and grape). For these stains, pour boiling water over the discolored area, cover with borax, and place in the sun. Peach stains can be removed by submerging the discolored area in cold water, cover with cream of tartar and set in the sun.

Should your hands become stained, try rubbing with cornmeal and vinegar (or try rubbing with lemon skins).

GRASS: To remove grass stains from white clothing, wash the stains with pure alcohol. This method may also be successful with colored fabrics, but first test a section of the material to see that the colors do not fade.

GREASE: Automobile grease and ordinary grease spots can be removed by soaking the material in hot water and then rubbing with tissue or some other absorbant cloth. Another method is to purchase some carbon tetrachloride. It is much cheaper than most commercial spot removers and is extremely effective in removing grease, oil and tar stains. If using this solvent, be sure to use in a well ventilated area and avoid inhaling the fumes.

Starch is also effective in removing grease stains. A bit of white starch moistened into a paste and applied to a grease spot (leave until dry and brush off), will work well for colorless grease or oil stains.

GUM: To remove gum that has stuck to a garment, hold an ice cube on the wrong side of the article directly under the gum. The ice will freeze the gum and make it possible to pick off.

INK: Ink stains which are often difficult to remove from fabrics may be removed by a simple home process. The stained article should be soaked in sour milk for a few hours and then rinsed with cold water. Red ink can be removed by covering the stain with freshly made mustard. Mix up a teaspoon of dry mustard with enough water to form a paste and rub on the stained area. If your hands should become stained, rub with a little household ammonia and rinse with clear water.

FLOORS

WAXING UNPOLISHED FLOORS: To wax floors that were never polished, the following method is good. The floors should first be washed thoroughly and dried. When dry, coat with some floor oil such as linseed oil. This should be at once rubbed with sawdust (which removes all surplus oil and polishes the floor). After this, any wax may be used according to directions and then, after a weighed brush is used, the old floor will be as smooth as new ones.

WAXING FLOORS: Hardwood floors should be waxed and polished once a month in order to keep them in good condition. First, dust your waxed floors or wipe them with a damp cloth wrung out of cool water. Then wax the floor.

PREVENT WORN SPOTS: Worn spots on polished floors in doorways or at the foot of stairs may be prevented by applying a thin coat of wax once or twice a month. Put the wax in cheesecloth and rub over the worn spots. Allow fifteen minutes for drying, then polish. In an hour or two apply a second coat of wax and polish.

SCRATCHED FLOORS: If your hardwood floors are soiled and badly scratched, scrub them with a good scouring powder and, when dry, rub in equal parts of linseed oil and turpentine. Let the floor dry. Next day wash and polish. Do not use scouring powder on floors with laquer finish.

173.

CRACKED FLOOR BOARDS: For filling cracks in floor, soak old newspapers in strong alum water until they form a soft pulp and press hard into the cracks. This method is more successful than using putty. When the hardened pulp is covered with paint or stain they will hardly show.

THRESHOLDS: Worn thresholds should always be rubbed with linseed oil and the oil should be allowed to dry for a day before varnish is put on.

MARKED FLOORS: If your hardwood floor is scarred with dark marks from rockers or furniture casters, rub the marks with very fine steel wool which has been dipped in very soapy water. Rinse and wax the area.

CLOSET FLOORS: A little turpentine on a cloth used to wipe out the floor of your clothes closet will serve as a warning to moths. Closet and bureau drawers may be treated in a like manner.

174.

MISCELLANEOUS HINTS

CANDLES: If you want candles to last longer try this: Take each candle by the wick and give it a good coat of varnish and then store the candles away for a day or two to harden. The varnish prevents the grease from running down and so preserves the life of the candle. Another method to lengthen candle life is to place the candles in the refrigerator for a few days before using. To make a candle fit any candle stick, dip the candle for a moment into very hot water. This will soften the wax so that it may be easily fitted into the candlestick.

CANE CHAIRS: When cane seats first begin to sag, rub them until throughly soaked with soap suds. Turn chair upside down and dry in the sun.

BEADS: When stringing beads or pearls of various sizes, place them in order on the grooves of a piece of corrugated paper. It will then be much easier to slip them on to the needle.

BROOMS: The life of a broom may be increased quite a bit and the task of sweeping made much easier if you form the habit of turning the broom after every few strokes so that the straw on each side of the handle is toward you an equal share of the time. As most of the wear is on the side toward you, the turning operation wears the straw down evenly all the way across. This habit gives you more sweeping area, it prevents the wearing down of the straw at one side and the curling up at the other side. The operation is performed quite unconsciously after the first two or three trials.

It is also important that brooms and all sweeping brushes be hung up when not in use. If left standing on the bristles, they will become bent and not do their work properly. If you have no place to hang them, stand them upside down.

SAVING BROOMS: Dip straw brooms in a bucket of water at least once a week. This will keep them clean and make them last longer.

BRUSHES: A brush may be easily ruined no matter what its quality. Among the don'ts are: Do not wash a brush in a strong alkaline or acid solution; do not dry it in an oven; do not permit it to remain wet longer than necessary; do not bend the bristles with your fingers; do not squeeze two brushes together. Sunlight is the best purifying agent. Good brushes come fairly high in price, but they are worth what you pay if you take proper care of them after each and every use.

SOFTENING PAINT BRUSHES: When paint brushes have become hardened and stiff through disuse, put some vinegar in an old can. Dilute it with one third boiling water and soak for about ten minutes. The brushes will come out soft and pliable unless you have been using something that hardens quite badly. There are chemicals on the market to renovate your brush but they also tend to destroy the bristles. Try the vinegar method first.

SHELLAC BRUSHES: Shellac brushes should be washed in denatured alcohol and then soap and water. Straighten the bristles and put the brushes away dry.

BRUSH FOR DUSTING: For dusting furniture, particularly if it is elaborate in design, there is nothing better than an ordinary paint brush. The bristles can not scratch the surface, and they remove the dust from the crannies better than a dust cloth possibly can.

CHAMOIS AS DUSTER: A piece of chamois that has been dampened makes an excellent duster. It makes furniture look like new. If the chamois becomes really stiff, rinse it in two quarts of lukewarm water with one teaspoon of olive oil added. This will make it quite soft. For a finger marked piano or other highly polished surfaces, try cold water and chamois skin. Have two skins, both very soft and pliable. Dip one in cold water, wring it very dry, and then wipe off the polished surface. Polish it with the dry skin.

DUSTLESS DUSTER: To make a dustless duster, take one yard of cheesecloth and wring it out in a pan of warm water to which has been added 1 ounce of oil of citronella and three tablespoons of denatured alcohol. Hang in air to dry.

USE GLOVES: Add a pair of gloves to the cleaning equipment and your hands will be kept looking and feeling well.

MOPS: Mops should be well shaken each time after use and occasionally should be renewed by soapsuds soaking. After the soaking, rinse in clear hot water and dry in the sun or a well ventilated area indoors. You may wish to fasten a hanger for your mop in the cleaning closet so that it may hang to dry and be kept away from the walls and floor in the cabinet.

RAGS: It takes half the drudgery from house cleaning to start with plenty of clean rags and brushes. A complete household equipment chest should include spiral brushes (bottle brushes) for cleaning the hard to get at places like wicker chairs and sink drains. Also a longhandled scrub brush to keep the hands out of dirty water and soft fiber brushes for shades, ceilings, moldings and polished floors. Rags are indispensable for cleaning spills, drying washed surfaces, wiping brushes, etc. When an article of clothing wears out, cut it up into squares suitable for being a rag.

PAINT: Buy a good quality paint that will cover and shine when worked into the wood. Don't paint in a hurry. It must be worked in well to give a fine finish and provide good wear. Use a soft brush which will not loose its bristles and remember it is better to use less paint on the brush to prevent drips.

KEEPING PAINT: Pour paraffin over paint left unused in a can and it will not harden. When ready to use, the wax seal will come out easily.

WASHING WALLS: Walls and delicate woodwork may be washed with water, white soap and a little ammonia added to the water. Be sure to change the water as soon as it becomes dirty.

PLASTER WALLS: Newly plastered walls should stand at least one week before being painted and much longer in damp weather. If it is not possible to allow the plaster to stand that long before finishing, wash the walls with a solution of zinc

178.

sulphate in the proportion of one pound of sulphate to a gallon of water (to neutralize the alkali in the plaster). If the plaster is not prepared in this manner, the alkali is likely to burn through and discolor the paint.

PAINTED WALLS:Before washing paint, wipe the dry dust off with a clean dry cloth. When washing, put a little household ammonia in warm water and use white soap. Change the water as often as it becomes dirty.

VARNISHED PAINT: Linseed oil is excellent for cleaning varnished grained paint. It should be applied with a piece of clean, soft flannel. Rub well and polish with a soft duster. Add only the very tiniest drop of oil.

CEILINGS: A bag of cotton flannel large enough to fit over the broom is a good method to clean ceilings and high walls. As soon as it is the least bit soiled, it can be removed, washed and put back again.

SMOKED CEILINGS: Smoked ceilings may be cleaned with warm water to which a bit of baking soda has been added.

WALLPAPER: You can make any wallpaper washable by going over it first with sizing and then using a clear shellac. This is advisable for the bathroom, kitchen and children's rooms. Should your wallpaper need repair, do not put on a square patch but cut the edges as nearly as possible to the pattern. If a plain paper, it is a good plan to tear it, as this makes a thinner edge which will stick better.

NAILS IN WALLS: Before driving nails for picture hooks into the wall, first see where the nails for baseboards are driven. Nails for baseboards are always driven in the studs. To prevent the plaster from chipping when driving a nail, heat the nail and it will go through smoothly.

CURTAINS: If washed curtains do not hang well after being laundered, slip a curtain rod through the bottom hem of each curtain and do not remove for a few days. At the end of that time the curtains will hang straight. If your window shades will not spring up quickly when pulled, take them down, hold firmly and with tweezers tighten the end spring.

BEADS: When stringing beads of various sizes, place them in order on the grooves of a piece of corrugated paper. It will then be much easier to slip them on the needle.

DRAFTS: Take a piece of material ¼ yard wide and as long as the door is wide, sew it up leaving one end open. Fill it with sawdust by using a fruit jar funnel. Do not fill it too full so you can pack it down to fit the corners. Place over the crack between the door and floor to keep out draft.

FIRES: Never throw waste paper on an open fire unless you watch it closely and be sure to replace the firescreen when you leave the room. Also, it is best to keep rugs away from the fireplace as a small flying ember can damage the rug and start a serious fire.

FIRE LOGS: A quick way to make fuel of newspapers is to take twelve single sheets and fold them twice, then again, and you will have a long narrow strip. Turn over so the open part is underneath and divide in three parts (unfolding the ends under into a bow knot). If all folds are well flattened, the bow knotting is easily and quickly done. Sheets must be used singly. Use five of them in place of the larger pieces of wood when starting a fire — two at each end and one in the middle. This saves wood and uses up the paper.

SPONGES: Have a few varieties of sponges on hand in the cleaning cabinet. There are quite a few varieties available and some you will find much more absorbant then others. Since synthetic sponges are much less expensive than natural ones, you should try a few different types to see which are suitable for your cleaning purposes.

WINDOWS: This is the easiest way to wash windows. Have one basin of warm water to which some household ammonia has been added. Use an ordinary cloth and wash windows thoroughly. Have another basin of clear, warm water. Into this dip a chamois, wring it dry as possible and go over the windos again. The chamois takes off the lint and water leaving the glass clear and shining. Another method is to use newspapers to wash and dry the glass. The newsprint will polish the glass and leave no lint behind. Be sure when washing windows that the sun is not shining directly on the glass as this can cause them to streak.

PAINT ON WINDOWS: Obstinate paint spots on windows may be removed by scraping with an old razor blade and then washing with ammonia water. The most stubborn paint marks on clothing or other fabric will yield to turpentine mixed with ammonia and rubbed into the spot. Hot strong vinegar will also remove paint and mortar from window glass.

DUSTING WINDOWS: The insides of the windows accumulate more dust than the outsides and if they are wiped off on the insides regurarly with a soft damp cloth they will not have to be washed so frequently.

WINDOW HINGES: If you have casement windows, be sure to oil the hinges occasionally. This helps prevent rust.

STICKY WINDOWS: If your windows do not run up easily, rub paraffin on the window cords and hand soap on the wood runners and you will notice an improvement.

WINDOW SCREENS: The brushes that can be attached to the end of a garden hose usually used for washing cars will be useful in washing window screens. Do not use too high a pressure with this.

FIREPLACE BRICKS: To clean fireplace bricks, cover them with a paste made of powdered pumice and household ammonia. Let it dry for an hour then scrub with warm soapy water.

FIREPLACE TILE: When the red tiles of the fireplace or porch floor become dull, rub them with a cut piece of lemon and salt. Then wash with warm soapy water.

FIREPLACE ASHES: Before cleaning a fireplace, sprinkle damp tea leaves over the ashes. This prevents the dust from rising and keeps the room clean.

BAMBOO FURNITURE: Bamboo furniture needs slightly different treatment from the ordinary hardwood articles. The fiber requires feeding from time to time in order to prevent excessive dryness. It should be rubbed regurarly with a mixture of linseed and turpentine applied with a flannel. Follow by a brisk polish with soft rags. Bamboo furniture should also be exposed as much as possible to the air and kept as far away from the fire as convenient.

WASHING WICKER: To wash wicker furniture, make a good suds of warm water and mild soap. Add a large pinch of salt. If there are any pieces especially soiled (or hard to reach), use a small scrubbing brush. Then rinse the whole piece well. Dry it thoroughly. A flannel cloth, which has a small amount of oil on it, should give the final polish.

WHITE FURNITURE: Dirt marks may be removed from white furniture with any good soap or cleansing powder. Ammonia used in the water turns white paint yellow.

White furniture may also be cleaned by dissolving baking soda in warm water. Apply the solution to the furniture with a soft cloth, rubbing with a dry one afterwards. Fingermarks and dirt are easily removed in this simple way. Use one teaspoon to a pint of water.

REED FURNITURE: To clean reed furniture, take it out of doors when the sun is warm, turn the garden hose on it and let it dry thoroughly before taking it into the house. If it is especially soiled, use a small bristle brush to clean the spots remaining.

BATHROOM CARE: Fifteen minutes daily care will keep your bathroom spotless. Air throughly, clean tub, handles, knobs and flush toilet with soap and water. Dust the floor, the woodwork and shelves. Once a week wipe the walls, ceiling, window shades, mirrors and lighting fixtures.

FAUCETS: Rubbing brass water faucets with furniture polish after cleaning will keep them bright. The oil in the polish prevents chemical action from splashing water.

BATHROOM WINDOWS: A good frosting for bathroom windows can be made by dissolving three teaspoons of epsom salts in a glass of water and adding one teaspoon of liquid glue. Stir well and apply to glass with brush.

CLOGGED PIPES: Clogged pipes may be cleaned in the following manner: Force a mixture of washing soda and salt (a handful of each) into the top of the pipe and leave for half an hour. Then pour down a kettleful of boiling water. A very narrow spiral brush available in most hardware stores is also excellent for removing trapped material near the mouth of the pipe. If this fails, there are numerous drain cleaners on the market which are much stronger. Consult your hardware store or market.

SHOPPING: Do not shop without first making out a list of things to be purchased. Do not shop after acquiring an aching head or jumpy nerves. If grocery shopping, eat first and you will avoid buying on impulse.

STAMPS: If postage stamps are glued together, lay a thin paper over them and run over it with a hot iron. The glue will not be hurt and the stamps will separate easily.

STOPPERS: To remove an obstinate stopper from a glass bottle, dip a piece of cloth into boiling water and wrap it tightly around the neck of the bottle. In a few minutes the stopper can be removed. If a cork has fallen into a bottle you wish to keep for future use, pour enough household ammonia into the bottle to float the cork. Let stand a few days and the cork will break into fine pieces allowing it to slide out of the bottle with ease.

WATER: Everyone should know where the water in the house can be shut off. Ceilings may be ruined while you are waiting for a plumber to mend a leaking pipe.

PASTE: An ideal substitute for paste is the white of an egg, or if you only need a small amount of pasting such as a postage stamp or an envelope, then simply wipe out the inside of an shell of a freshly broken egg and you have a paste that sticks like glue.

HOT WATER BAGS: Fill hot water bags about half full of water and then squeeze out the air before screwing in the top. This keeps them hot longer. Never, however, fill a hot water bottle from a boiling tea kettle. Water that is too hot is harmful to a rubber bottle. Use water from 150 to 160 degrees fahrenheit and pour it from a pitcher into the bottle. Should the bottle leak, try inner tube patches to seal the leak.

LOCKS: Dipping keys in oil occasionally will keep locks in order.

OLIVE OIL: Olive oil may be used in more ways than salad dressing. As a toilet accessory, it is extremely useful. The oil should be of pure Italian sort. Heated, it makes an excellent bath for the hands and elbows, smoothing away any roughness. A weekly fifteen minutes soak in hot olive oil has a beneficial effect on fingernails. Afterward, the cuticle should be pushed back with an orangewood stick and the nails manicured as usual. Hot olive oil is beneficial to the scalp and is good for either oiliness or dryness. It should be rubbed in at night prior to the shampoo.

GARDENING: Working in the garden makes the hands grimy and hard. About half a teaspoon of ordinary moist sugar rubbed into the hands with a soapy lather will clean them and leave them smooth.

186.

INDEX